FASHIONARY

ISBN 978-988-77111-3-1
SN TDMV112206CB

Designed and published in Hong Kong
By Fashionary International Ltd
Printed in China

The Denim Manual is an ongoing project.
If you have any feedback, please don't hesitate to send it to
feedback@fashionary.org

 @fashionary
 @fashionary
 @fashionary

Fashionary Team 2022

THE

DENIM

MANUAL

A COMPLETE VISUAL GUIDE
· FOR THE ·

Denim Industry

CONTENTS

PREFACE

Denim is a complex and special fabric with a rich
historical and cultural heritage. What makes it so
different from other fabrics is its adaptability and
versatility; there are endless ways to tint, fade, distress,
embellish and customise it, and each method creates
a unique outcome.

It is important, but challenging, for designers to
understand how each process works.
Many of the existing resources focus only on style and
design; technological guidelines are often too difficult
for beginners; and, while there is an abundance of
information, it is scattered, incomplete and
often contradictory.

In this comprehensive book, we will explore the
meaning and value of denim throughout history, as
well as illustrate and explain every aspect of practical
knowledge, expertise and terminology in a concise and
easy-to-read manner.

With the assistance of experts and industry insiders,
we at Fashionary have developed the content and tips
in The Denim Manual to address the unique needs
of denim designers. We hope the book will give you a
thorough understanding of the denim industry, and
guide you through your own design journey.

DENIM FAQs

< **DENIM FABRIC** >

1. Is all denim 100% cotton?

No. Only traditional denim is 100% cotton. After the 1960s, denim manufacturers began producing blended-fiber denim.
Today, denim can be made from many types of fibers, weave structures, colors and yarns.

For more details on denim — *see p.032*

2. What is the difference between raw denim and pre-washed denim?

Raw denim is unwashed or untreated denim; it is also known as "dry denim."
Pre-washed denim has been washed or treated; pre-washing can also be called "pre-distressing."
Pre-washed denim is usually softer, and has a faded look.

For more details on raw denim — *see p.046*
For pre-washed denim — *see p.136*

3. Why is selvage denim more expensive than regular denim?

Selvage denim is produced by traditional shuttle looms, which are old and require frequent maintenance; the process is more time-consuming and less productive, and therefore more expensive.

For more details on selvage denim — *see p.048*

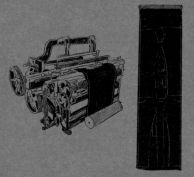

4. Why is denim so heavy? Is there such a thing as lightweight denim?

Because denim was originally made for work clothing, it needed to be very durable. The fabric had to be heavy to resist friction and breakage. However, today there are many lightweight denims available.

For more details on denim weight — *see p.068*

INDIGO DYE

5. Why is denim indigo blue?

Blue was the color of the working class in the 18th century; so, because denim was originally made for workwear, it was dyed blue. Also, at that time, natural indigo was readily available, making it the major type of dye used for denim.

For more details about indigo dyes — see p.038

6. Does natural indigo have antibacterial properties?

Yes, studies indicate that natural indigo shows antimicrobial activity against microorganisms. In fact, many other natural dyes also have antimicrobial properties – but none are suitable for medical use.

7. Do all denim garments fade? And why?

Yes. Basically, all indigo denim garments will fade after washing.

Since the yarns are immersed in indigo only briefly during the dyeing process, the dye does not reach the center of the yarn completely. Therefore, when it is washed or under friction, it will gradually fade and part of the yarn's white core will be exposed.

USING DENIM

8. What do I need to know before sewing denim?

I. **Needle:** Choose the correct size of needle for the weight and thickness of the fabric; the heavier the denim, the thicker the needle should be.

II. **Thread:** Choose a) the right thickness of thread, for durability, and b) the correct fiber. Cotton / polyester blended thread is strong and has better abrasion resistance. Also, polyester does not absorb dyes like natural fibers. So most jeans use cotton/polyester blended thread.

III. **Machine:** Use heavy-duty sewing machines to sew medium or heavyweight denim, and ordinary sewing machines for lightweight denim.

IV. **Setting:** Adjust the tension and stitch length to avoid wrinkles in the seams.

9. Are the holes in ripped denim made by hand or machine?

The holes can be made either way. Scissors, knives and tweezers can be used to create rips and holes by hand.

As for machine-made holes, different grinders are usually used in the factory; they speed up the ripping, tearing and distressing process.

For more details about distressing process — see p.126

10. What is denim on denim?

Denim on denim is also called double denim. This means pairing a denim top (or jacket) with a denim bottom (jeans) to create an overall denim look.

11. Can denim garments be made to measure?

Yes, there is customized denim clothing on the market.

Some luxury brands and tailoring shops provide this service, and customers can choose everything from the cut and color to the wash, closure and stitching. Custom-made denim clothing is usually more expensive than mass-produced garments.

DENIM CARE / MAINTENANCE

12. Is there a way to prevent the holes in jeans from ripping more?

There are several ways to preserve the holes in ripped jeans:
I. Use iron-on denim patches on both sides of the hole.
II. Sew around the holes by hand or with a sewing machine to keep them from growing.

13. What's the best way to avoid shrinkage when washing denim?

Buying pre-shrunk denim will help prevent serious shrinkage in the first wash. Also avoid washing denim in hot water or drying it in a hot dryer. Instead, wash it in cold water on a gentle cycle.

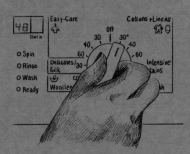

14. How can I prevent denim dye from bleeding?

Use the same method you'd use to avoid shrinkage: do not wash denim frequently; follow the care instructions on the label; turn denim clothing inside out before washing; use a special denim detergent; and finally, wash denim in cold water using the gentle cycle.

For more details on denim care — see p.184

15. Is it possible to restore color to faded jeans?

Yes. You can re-dye denim clothing to make it darker. Remember to cover any leather patches to protect them from the dye. Also note that Lycra and polyester will not absorb the dye, while cotton and linen will.

For more details about overdyeing — see p.172

16. I've heard freezing jeans will remove odors. Does it work?

Not really. It won't kill all the bacteria in the denim; it will only slow their growth. The dormant bacteria will regenerate once the jeans come out of the freezer.
Scientific evidence shows that laundering denim is a better way to kill bacteria.

17. How can I get rid of that vintage denim smell?

There are several ways to eliminate the smell without washing. They include sealing the item in a lidded container along with activated charcoal, baking soda or coffee grounds.
Fresh air and sunshine also are great natural deodorizers.

FACTS

18. Are there any denim museums?

Yes, there are several denim museums. They've been established by both individuals and well-known manufacturers and companies.
One of them is the Levi Strauss Museum in Buttenheim, Germany. It is located in the house where Levi Strauss was born,
shows the evolution of Levi Strauss jeans, and features displays of historical jeans.
The other one, The Jeans Museum in Zürich, Switzerland, displays more than 14,000 items of denim clothing from the 1950s to the present.

19. Do vintage jeans have investment value?

Yes, but not many are very valuable. Usually the older and more original an item is, the more valuable it is – especially jeans produced before the 1970s, and denim garments by Levi's and other famous brands.
A Japanese collector bought four pairs of old jeans for USD908 (100,000 yen). Experts later appraised and confirmed their value at USD9084 (1 million yen); it's estimated that the jeans were worn by a miner in Los Angeles during the Gold Rush.

20. Why does vintage denim smell?

When you buy denim from a second-hand store, it often carries a distinct, musty smell from many sources: mildew, damp, mothballs and other lingering scents including cigarettes and perfume worn by the previous owners.

21. What are the most expensive jeans in the world?

In 2008, a pair of jeans by the brand Secret Circus sold for USD1.3 million; the price reflects the 15 high-quality diamonds on the right back pocket. The jeans were handmade in Los Angeles and embellished with diamonds cut by London jewelry company Duttson Rocks.

HOW DENIM GARMENTS ARE MADE

THE STEPS THAT GO INTO THEIR DEVELOPMENT, CREATION AND MARKETING

PRODUCT DEVELOPMENT

FASHION DESIGNER

PATTERN MAKER

GRAPHIC DESIGNER

SAMPLING / PRODUCTION MERCHANDISER

SAMPLE MAKING

FABRIC CUTTER

SEWING-MACHINE OPERATOR

FABRIC / TRIM DEVELOPMENT

SOURCING MERCHANDISER
Responsible for sourcing fabric and trims

WASHING DEPARTMENT

WASH TECHNICIAN
Responsible for wet and dry processes

INSPECTION DEPARTMENT

QUALITY CONTROLLER

FINISHING DEPARTMENT

FINISHING WORKER
Responsible for the last stage: ironing, thread cutting,
trims and embellishments

TRD. DENIM MRK.
throughout
THE DECADES

EST. 1871

The history of denim goes back to the 1600s, when cotton, wool, linen and silk-blend twills were made in France and Italy. In the 1700s, textile mills were emerging in America, and the first "waist overalls" (what we now call jeans) became a workwear staple for laborers. At that time, denim clothing was primarily worn by men; women started wearing it around World War I. Denim is woven into countless historical eras including the Gold Rush, labor and social-justice movements, and subcultures of all kinds. Today, denim's allure is universal and multifaceted. Not only is it durable and practical, it also represents rugged individualism, rebellion, freedom and sexuality.

BLUE: THE COLOR OF THE WORKING CLASS

Laborers wear durable blue workwear provided by their employers; blue is the cheapest color to produce. Even today, the term "blue-collar" refers to someone who does manual labor.

THE TERM "BLUE JEANS"

"Bleu de Gênes" ("blue from Genoa") is a durable, coarse fabric manufactured in Genoa, Italy and worn by manual laborers.

1600s — 1700s — 1800s

THE ORIGINS OF DENIM

SERGE DE NÎMES

A sturdy twill fabric called "serge de Nîmes" ("twill from Nîmes"), made in the south of France, evolves into the English word "denim." There are some doubts about the origins of the word, however. Some believe it comes from another French fabric called "nim." Confusing matters further, both fabrics – serge de Nîmes and nim – are originally made from wool or a wool / silk blend, unlike today's denim, which is cotton.

AMERICAN COTTON TWILL

Textile mills in the United States start making the same twill fabric as European denim; they use local cotton because it is more readily available.

INDIGO FROM INDIA

Indigo dye, imported from India, becomes popular in the European textile trade.

JACOB YOUPHES

Jacob Youphes is born in Latvia.

1854

After emigrating to the United States, Youphes changes his surname to Davis and starts a tailoring business.

1869

Davis moves to Reno, Nevada. There, he makes tents, horse blankets and wagon covers in heavy-duty cotton duck and denim purchased from Levi Strauss in San Francisco.

STRAUSS AND DAVIS JOIN FORCES

Davis seeks a partner to help him mass-produce waist overalls, so he writes a letter to his fabric supplier, Levi Strauss. The two become business partners.

1848-1855: THE GOLD RUSH	The Gold Rush begins in California. Large mining companies arrive in the race to extract gold and minerals, and miners need supremely hard-wearing and durable clothes.

1829   1831   MID-1800s   1871   1872

LEVI STRAUSS

Loeb Strauss is born in Bavaria.

1847

Strauss moves to New York to start a dry-goods business.

1850s

Strauss changes his first name to Levi.

1853

During the San Francisco Gold Rush, Strauss opens a wholesale house selling dry goods; one of the products he sells is denim fabric.

WAIST OVERALLS

A local worker asks Davis to make sturdy pants for her husband. Davis uses white cotton duck, and adds metal rivets to the corners of the pockets to prevent tearing, thereby making the garment last longer.

1873
LEVI STRAUSS & CO.

Strauss and Davis patent their pants on May 20.

THE LEE BRAND

Henry David Lee and four business partners establish a mercantile company in Salinas, Kansas, that sources and distributes dry goods and groceries. Later, in 1912, Lee opens its first garment factory to produce overalls and work jackets.

LEVI'S 501 JEANS

The brand's original riveted blue denim jeans are named after their lot number: 501.

DENIM JACKET

The first denim jacket is made by Levi Strauss & Co.

1880   1889   1890   1897   19

MASS MARKETING

Waist overalls are mass produced and come in two options: blue denim or brown cotton duck. The denim version catches on. Typically worn by men, the style is popular among miners and laborers.

SYNTHETIC INDIGO

Synthetic indigo is developed, and is soon widely used in the textile industry.

LEE BIB OVERALLS

Lee makes its first bib overalls from lightweight 8oz denim. They become hugely popular.

FREEDOM-ALLS

Levi's introduces its first women's garment, Freedom-Alls. They consist of a belted cotton tunic and harem pants.

CHAIN STORES

Retailers such as JC Penney and Sears start selling jeans at lower prices than small, independent local shops.

LEE 101 JEANS

Lee launches its first cowboy pants, 101 jeans, made from heavy 13oz denim. They are designed to meet the needs of cowboys and rodeo riders.

1911   1913   1918   **1920**   1924

1914-1918: WWI: WAIST OVERALLS FOR WOMEN After men are drafted to fight in the war, women enter the workforce and begin wearing waist overalls.

UNION-ALLS

Inspired by car mechanics, Lee designs Union-Alls, a one-piece garment that incorporates waist overalls and a jacket, and protects the wearer's clothes.

BUDDY LEE

Lee creates Buddy Lee, a promotional doll dressed in mini overalls, to establish the brand's unique position in the market and stimulate sales.

ZIPPER-FLY JEANS

Lee starts selling the world's first zipper-fly jeans, model 101Z. The brand was the first to use "hookless fasteners" on jeans, coveralls and playsuits.

SANFORIZED DENIM

American businessman Sanford Lockwood Cluett patents a process to reduce shrinkage in denim and make it softer. Sanforized denim becomes popular with mass-market jeans brands.

LEVI'S FOR WOMEN

Levi's introduces Lady Levi's – its first women's jeans – which soon become part of the Dude Ranch Duds line. The jeans are specially designed for the female body.

DENIM IN *VOGUE*

Vogue features Lady Levi's in an article about dude ranches, and Levi Strauss & Co. runs an ad in the magazine that states, "true Western chic was invented by cowboys."

1927   1930   1934   1935

1929–1939: THE GREAT DEPRESSION

While unemployment and poverty cripple the nation, movies, photographs and murals depicting denim-clad cowboys, factory workers and farmers transform Americans' perception of denim. It becomes a symbol of pride, and shorthand for the nation's industriousness, tenacity, frontier spirit, and triumph over adversity.

THE COWBOY CRAZE

Western films and novels popularize cowboy culture; the public begins to emulate the rugged actors who wear denim in the movies.

BIG CUFFS

Jeans from this period are made of unsanforized denim that shrinks when washed. Customers therefore buy their jeans slightly too big, and often need to roll up the long cuffs. Cowboys soon start using the cuffs as storage pockets for tobacco and the like; on horseback, it is easier for them to reach into a cuff than a saddlebag.

HOLLYWOOD

Katharine Hepburn is the first actress to wear denim pants in a major motion picture.

THE TEEN MARKET

Music and movies add cultural cachet to denim. Marlon Brando and James Dean become rebel icons with their boxy, cuffed denim trousers. Teenagers start calling waist overalls "jeans."

39-1945:
ARTIME
EMAND

The U.S. military purchases denim workwear for its servicemen; women entering the workforce also begin wearing more denim. Due to shortages, civilian clothing prices rise.

1940 — 1945 — 1947 — 1950 — 1951

WOMEN NEED WORKWEAR

During WWII, American women are again called upon to work in factories and do manual labor. Denim-clad women like Rosie the Riveter become a powerful symbol of the war effort.

Wrangler

WRANGLER JEANS

Introduced by the Blue Bell Overall Company, Wrangler jeans are endorsed by rodeo cowboys.

SIDE-ZIP JEANS

Levi's reintroduces women's jeans with a side zip; they are very popular. Wrangler had launched its first women's zip-up jeans in 1948.

THE CANADIAN TUXEDO

Actor and crooner Bing Crosby is denied entrance to a Vancouver hotel because he is wearing Levi's jeans; the brand makes a custom denim tuxedo jacket for him after the incident. The term "Canadian tuxedo" is used to describe his head-to-toe denim outfit.

SCHOOLS BAN JEANS

Many schools prohibit students from wearing denim in the classroom. It is considered disrespectful, and a form of rebellion against authority.

FIT FOR ROYALTY

Princess Alexandra of Kent – Queen Elizabeth II's first cousin – becomes the first member of the British royal family to be photographed wearing jeans.

BLACK DENIM

Wrangler, a division of the Blue Bell Overall Company, popularizes black denim, and produces the outfit worn by TV cowboy Hopalong Cassidy, played by actor William Boyd.

**1955-1968:
THE CIVIL RIGHTS MOVEMENT**

Denim becomes a symbol of protest in the struggle for black freedom. Activists reclaim the fabric, wearing de jeans, overalls and jackets to symbolize the work cloth worn by slaves and poor sharecroppers.

1954   1957   LATE 1950s   1960s

MARILYN MONROE

The actress wears high-waisted slim-cut jeans in the movie "River of No Return."

RIGHT FOR SCHOOL!

LEVI'S
AMERICA'S FINEST OVERALL SINCE 1850

A CLEAN-CUT IMAGE

Denim and cotton companies form a committee to transform denim's image. They create ads promoting jeans as "right for school" and depicting young people in dungarees as model citizens, not rebels.

NYLON

For the first time, nylon is used to add stretch to women's jeans.

ROCK 'N' ROLL

During the 1960s, rock 'n' roll becomes a huge influence on fashion, with many musicians wearing denim.

HIGH-LOW DRESSING

In the movie "Breakfast at Tiffany's," Audrey Hepburn wears jeans in the "Moon River" scene – it is a stark contrast to the designer clothing she wears in the rest of the film.

COLORED JEANS

By the early 60s, jeans are available in a variety of colors. Wrangler introduces a women's range in multiple shades.

DENIM SKIRTS

The denim skirt is born in the 70s as a way to reuse old and damaged jeans.

SYNTHETIC BLENDS

Jeans become stretchy and more lightweight when synthetic fibers are added to cotton.

1967

1970

1976

1977

HIPPIES AND THE COUNTERCULTURE

Jeans styles diversify to include boot-cut, bell-bottom, patches, embroidery, paint and other types of embellishment. These become the uniform of the hippie movement.

DOUBLE DENIM

Double denim – also known as denim on denim – becomes popular. Sonny and Cher help kick-start the trend, which is also popular among off-duty musicians and bohemian celebrities.

CALVIN KLEIN

Calvin Klein is the first designer brand to show jeans on the catwalk.

THE CHRISTOPHER STREET LOOK

Gay culture has a huge influence on mainstream fashion. Tight, skinny jeans – a staple of gay men's wardrobes – are soon embraced by the rest of the world.

DIESEL

The Italian clothing brand, founded by Adriano Goldschmied and Renzo Rosso, sells mostly denim clothing.

DAISY DUKES

Cut-off denim short shorts are worn by the character Daisy Duke on American TV show "The Dukes of Hazzard." Thereafter, the shorts are known as "Daisy Dukes."

RIPS, TEARS AND FRAYS

Hippies, punks and metal-heads all embrace ripped jeans. Soon, designer brands including Vivienne Westwood and D&G feature the heavily distressed aesthetic in their collections.

LATE 1970s

1978

1979

1980

PUNK ROCK

Countercultures still hold sway over jeans trends. Punk rock and other music subcultures inspire snow-wash denim, which is often paired with tighter and darker jeans.

JEANS GO PRESIDENTIAL

American President Jimmy Carter – a former peanut farmer – reveals that he wears denim at the White House. Later, Presidents Ronald Reagan, Bill Clinton, George W. Bush and Barack Obama also don denim while off-duty.

DESIGNER JEANS

Chic, Calvin Klein, Gloria Vanderbilt, Jordache and others usher in an era of high-priced designer jeans.

CHANEL'S DENIM SUIT

Karl Lagerfeld shows a denim suit in his collection for the house of Chanel.

THE JOHN HUGHES EFFECT

John Bender (played by Judd Nelson) wears a denim jacket in the John Hughes movie "The Breakfast Club," highlighting the character's hard-luck, working-class back story. The jacket and the character become icons of 80s high-school angst.

VOGUE COVER

Jeans appear on the cover of the November 1988 issue of *Vogue*. The model wears Guess stonewashed jeans and a Christian Lacroix jacket; the mixing of denim with couture is a highly controversial move by *Vogue* editor Anna Wintour.

1982

MID-1980s

1985

1988

1989

THE FALL OF THE BERLIN WALL

Thousands of jubilant young people dressed in denim clothing – once a symbol of Western capitalism and decadence – celebrate the fall of the Berlin Wall and their newfound freedom.

WHITE JEANS

Popularized by Wham!, white jeans are all the rage.

BUTTON-FLY MANIA

Levi's button-fly jeans are on the rise, eventually becoming more popular than zipper-fly jeans.

CINDY CRAWFORD'S SHORTS

The model wears denim shorts in a TV commercial for Pepsi cola.

HIGH-WAISTED JEAN

In the hit TV series "Beverly Hills, 90210," the female characters wear high-waisted, ankle-length jeans; in 2008, they're referred to as "Mom jeans."

LASERS

The first laser-distressing technology for denim garments is developed by a Florida company.

1990 1991 1992 1993 1994

GRUNGE

Grunge music and its subculture exert a huge influence on fashion: long, messy hair, flannel shirts, distressed jeans and combat boots make the leap from Seattle to the rest of the world.

LOW-RISE

Madonna wears low-rise butt-grazing jeans in an ad for MTV, giving the style a sales boost.

HIP-HOP

Hip-hop overtakes grunge as the most influential subculture: oversized denim jackets, baggy jeans and double denim are its signature style. Soon the look is ubiquitous among teens and adults alike.

BOOT-CUT

Boot-cut jeans are popular again – but they're straighter than before.

DOUBLE DENIM REDUX

Britney Spears and Justin Timberlake make a red-carpet appearance wearing matching all-denim ensembles.

CAPRIS

Echoing 50s and 60s pedal pushers, Capri pants make a comeback – this time in denim.

1995   **2000**   **2001**   **2003**   **2005**

BLING

Brands embellish jeans with crystals, studs and other sparkly elements.

SUPER-LOW

Keira Knightley wears super-low-rise jeans on the red carpet. Soon, the 2" zipper is de rigueur.

PRINTS AND PATTERNS

Denim splashes out: colors, patterns and animal prints start trending.

BOXY TO BOYFRIEND

The boxy jeans of the 60s are rebranded for women as boyfriend jeans. They are loose-fitting, cuffed and often distressed.

SMART JACKET

Levi's collaborates with Jacquard by Google on a Trucker jacket with a built-in sensor that syncs with the wearer's other devices.

2008   2009   2010s   2016

DENIM BRANDS BEGIN TO EXPLORE SUSTAINABLE PRACTICES

JEGGINGS

A comfortable cross between jeans and leggings, jeggings appear in retail stores.

ORGANIC

Swedish brand Nudie Jeans creates a 100% organic denim collection.

BIODEGRADABLE STRETCH DENIM

Coreva, patented by Candiani Denim, uses a plant-based yarn to replace synthetic petrol-based yarns, creating a biodegradable stretch denim fabric.

RELAXED SILHOUETTES

Denim moves toward more relaxed and voluminous silhouettes, including baggy jeans, flares and streetwear styles.

TWO-TONE

Two-tone denim is seen on celebs, models and cool girls – especially during Fashion Week.

2017   2019   2020   2021

FRAYED EDGES

A new take on distressed denim, frayed hems go from street style to mainstream.

SELVAGE & RAW

Retro-style raw and selvage denim achieve cult status.

BACK TO THE 80S

80s silhouettes – including high waists, tapered legs and knee-high boots – are seen on the catwalk.

ECRU

Ecru jeans – part of the head-to-toe neutrals trend – emerge as an environmentally friendly alternative to white jeans.

SUSTAINABILITY

Denim brands focus on not damaging the environment; many use sustainable materials and methods that use less water and electricity, and fewer chemicals.

Denim

THE FABRIC

★ ★ ★

CERTIFIED — INDIGO

MADE OF COTTON

Denim is one of the most popular and most
durable fabrics in the world. Traditionally,
denim was a blue fabric made of cotton in a
twill weave, and was yarn-dyed with indigo.
Nowadays there are numerous types of
denim on the market. In addition, different
surface finishing is used, such as coating and
printing. These increase the functionality
and aesthetics, and add value to the denim.

DENIM FABRIC:
CHARACTERISTICS ᴼᶠ TRADITIONAL DENIM

TWILL STRUCTURE
1 weft yarn passes under 2 or more warp yarns to create a diagonal pattern on the surface of the fabric.

STURDINESS
Durable and tear-resistant due to the highly twisted yarn.

INDIGO WARP YARN
Indigo-dyed warp yarn (vertical) with white weft yarn (horizontal).

FADING
Blue shades fade or whiten over time due to wearing and washing.

01 CLEANING COTTON FIBERS

Opening, cleaning and removing debris and dust from the cotton fiber.

02 BLENDING/MIXING

Combining various grades or different types of fiber to yield the desired properties.

03 SPINNING

Fibers are drawn out and twisted together to form yarn.

For further details, see *Page 034*

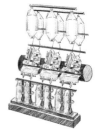

04 WARPING

Transferring the yarns from different cones forms a sheet of yarn on a warp beam.

05 DYEING

The warp yarns are dyed in indigo.

For further details, see *Page 041*

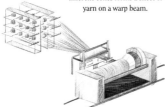

DENIM FROM FIBER TO FABRIC

06 BEAMING

Winding the dyed rope of yarns parallel over the beam in a sheet form.

07 SIZING

Treating warp yarns with protective coating to reduce abrasion during the weaving process.

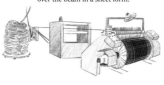

08 WEAVING

Interlacing warp and weft yarns into a twill.

09 FINISHING

Applying wet or dry treatments to change the appearance, feel or performance of the fabric.

For further details, see *Page 062*

10 PACKING

Packing can take various forms, such as rolling or folding.

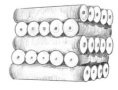

TWO YARN-SPINNING METHODS

Spinning is the process of producing yarn from fibers. There are two spinning methods commonly used to produce yarn for denim, and these affect the characteristics of the resulting fabric.

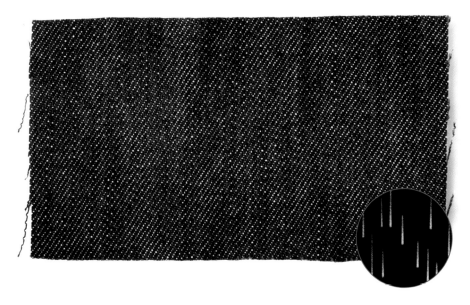

RING DENIM
Ring denim is made using ring-spun yarn for the warp.

RING SPINNING

Characteristics
· Produces stronger, softer yarn
· Finer, but less uniform
· Produces more variations, such as slubs
· Can produce multi-core yarn, such as elastic yarn

Fiber
Usually produced from long fibers

Background
Ring-spinning is one of the oldest spinning methods. The ring-spinning machine was invented in the United States in 1828; most denim manufacturers used the ring spinning method until the late 1970s.

Method
Raw fiber is placed into roving frames to reduce the mass, then twisted for strength; the resulting yarn is wound onto a bobbin.

Production speed
Slower

Production cost
Higher

<table>
<tr><td>

RING DENIM vs.
RING X RING DENIM

</td><td>

Ring denim uses ring-spun yarn only for the warp.
Ring x ring denim uses ring-spun yarn for both the
warp and weft yarns.

</td></tr>
</table>

OE (OPEN-END) DENIM
OE denim is made using rotor-spun yarn in the warp or weft (or both).

ROTOR SPINNING

Characteristics
· Produces weaker, coarser yarn
· Fuzzier, but more uniform
· Produces fewer variations, such as
a salt-and-pepper effect
· Cannot produce multi-core yarn

Fiber
Usually produced from short fibers

Background
Rotor spinning is also called open-end
spinning. Developed in the 1970s, it was
quickly adopted by denim manufacturers,
and became popular because it is more
economical.

Method
Yarn is spun directly from slivers, using a
spinning rotor and a withdrawal system
that compacts the fibers into yarn.

Production speed
Up to 5 times faster than ring spinning

Production cost
Lower

HOW YARNS AFFECT DENIM

A yarn's count, torsion and slubs will affect the weight, strength, appearance, hand-feel, texture and color of denim. The yarn count for denim ranges from Ne.1.6 to Ne.60; the most common yarn counts for denim are 7 and 8.

YARN COUNT

LOW YARN COUNT   **HIGH YARN COUNT**

Thicker	**Appearance**	Finer
Heavier (Ne.7, approx. 13oz)	**Fabric weight**	Lighter (Ne.20, approx. 6oz)
Thicker	**Thickness**	Thinner
Coarse	**Hand feel**	Softer

| | TORSION | |

HIGHER TWIST		**LOWER TWIST**
Produces stronger denim as it has higher torsion	**Fabric strength**	Produces weaker denim
Stiffer	**Hand feel**	Softer
Less indigo dye can be absorbed	**Color absorption**	More indigo dye can be absorbed

| | SLUBS | |

SLUB YARN		**NO-SLUB YARN**
Irregular	**Thickness**	Consistent
· Uneven in appearance · Produces vertical fades after washing	**Texture**	· Flatter appearance · Fades evenly

INDIGO DYES

Indigo, usually used for dyeing denim, is one of the oldest dyes in textile history. Natural indigo is made from plants, and is expensive and time-consuming. Therefore, synthetic indigo is widely used in the fashion industry.

THE ORIGINS OF INDIGO
Indigo originally came from India and was first supplied to Europe in the Greco-Roman era. The name comes from "indikón" in Greek.

NATURAL INDIGO

INDIGOFERA TINCTORIA
The most widely used of all indigo plants, it is also called "Indigofera" and is usually cultivated in tropical and subtropical regions.

ISATIS TINCTORIA (WOAD)
An important source throughout Europe, it spread from the Mediterranean to northern Europe.

POLYGONUM TINCTORIUM
Commonly known as Chinese indigo or Japanese indigo, it is normally cultivated in subtropical regions.

LONCHOCARPUS CYANESCENS
A traditional source of indigo in West Africa, it is also known as "Yoruba indigo" (or *elu* in Yoruba).

HOW NATURAL INDIGO IS MADE
The water extraction method, from leaves to powder

01
PLANTING & GROWING
Indigo plants can be grown from seed, or propagated. It needs full sun to grow.

02
HARVESTING
Indigo plants should be harvested before the flowers open. To keep the plant alive, only half of the leaves are picked.

03
SOAKING
The leaves are pressed with stones in a vat, then pure water is added. The vat is covered and left for at least 24 hours.

04
ALKALIZATION
Slaked lime is gently mixed into the water.

05
OXIDATION
Air is whisked into the liquid, which changes the water from green to indigo blue.

06
DRYING
The pigment is filtered out using a silk screen, then dried in the sun.

SYNTHETIC INDIGO

Synthetic indigo is more stable, more uniform in color, and easier to control, allowing higher productivity and lower costs. The chemical structure of indigo was formulated by German chemist Adolf von Baeyer in 1883; it began to be used commercially in 1897. By 1913, synthetic indigo had almost replaced natural indigo.

Adolf von Baeyer

NATURAL INDIGO		SYNTHETIC INDIGO
Distinctive green cast	**Appearance**	Red cast, some purple blue (A green cast can be created when mixed with sulfur dye)
· Inconsistent color (A more uniform color can be created through multiple dyeing, but it is costly) · Fades more slowly · Softer and less contrast fading	**Dye extraction**	· More uniform color · Faster and higher contrast fading
Higher (More natural indigo is needed to achieve darker and more uniform tones)	**Production cost**	Lower

DYEING METHODS

Today there are three main dyeing methods used in the textile industry. Different methods produce different results. Most denim is yarn-dyed.

YARN DYEING

APPEARANCE
The front of the fabric is colored, while the back is not.

BACKGROUND
Most denim is yarn-dyed. The yarn is dyed before it is woven into fabric. Traditionally, the warp yarn is dyed with indigo, while the weft yarn is undyed.

PIECE DYEING

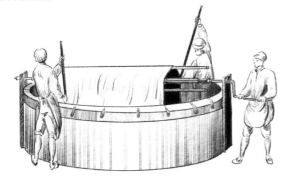

APPEARANCE
Color shows on both sides.

BACKGROUND
Piece dyeing is also known as fabric dyeing. The fabric is dyed after it has been woven. This method is rarely used in mass production because the result can be uneven and unstable. However, it can work well for individual brands.

GARMENT DYEING

APPEARANCE
Color shows on both sides.

BACKGROUND
Garment dyeing is the dyeing of semi-finished or fully finished garments. It is used to create different patterns, lines, and colors on denim garments. The garment can by dyed by different techniques, including tie-dyeing.

YARN DYEING

Yarn-dyeing is the traditional method of dyeing denim; the process of dyeing warp yarns with indigo is considered key to denim manufacturing. Darker shades of denim require multiple dye processes.

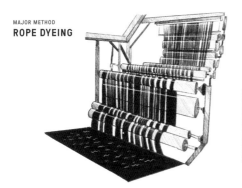

MAJOR METHOD
ROPE DYEING

PROCESS

The yarns are twisted into rope form; they then undergo a repetitive sequence of dipping and oxidation. The number of sequences will determine how dark the indigo shade is.

PROS	CONS
· Most popular indigo dyeing technique · More even and stable in color · Higher productivity	· Requires more space for machinery · Less flexible when changing color

---

MAJOR METHOD
SLASHER DYEING / SHEET DYEING

PROCESS

Yarns are passed through multiple warp beams and several baths of indigo dye before being sized and wound in preparation for weaving. This method combines dyeing and sizing into one process.

PROS	CONS
· More flexible when changing color · Requires less space	· Less even and less uniform* in color * Mechanical improvements have been developed by some denim manufacturers.

ALTERNATIVE METHOD
HANK DYEING

PROCESS

Skeins of yarn are placed on hooks and washed, which loosens the fibers so they can absorb the dye. The process is repeated several times: the yarn is dipped into the dye for up to 2 days, washed, and re-dipped. Once the desired color has been achieved, the yarn is steamed to fix the dye to the fibers.

PROS	CONS
· Maximum color penetration · The color is richer than other techniques · Less damage to the yarn · Yarn remains soft	· Time-consuming

DYEING AGENTS <u>AND</u> APPLICATIONS

In addition to indigo, changing fashion trends have led to different types of dye being applied to denim. As a result, modern denim can be found in a variety of shades and variations.

	INDIGO	SULFUR
Original		
Dark wash		
Medium wash		
Light wash		
Cross-section view of yarn	*Indigo* / *White core*	*Sulfur*
Background	Indigo is the most traditional and popular dyestuff for yarn dyeing.	Sulfur is the second most popular dyestuff for denim.
Color (Raw appearance)	Indigo produces a brilliant blue color, usually with a red or purplish cast; it's also known as red-cast denim.	Sulfur results in dull and deep shades in a limited range of tones including black, blue, khaki and green.
Washed appearance	The indigo will gradually fade after washing.	The range of shades after washing is not as wide as indigo.
Common application	Blue denim	Black denim, colored denim

SULFUR TOP

Sulfur dye is applied after indigo dye.

Sulfur top dye usually produces a gray or green cast of denim, such as vintage green-cast.

Denim becomes more blue with every wash, because indigo is the base layer (the sulfur gets washed away).

Blue-black, green-cast, gray-cast denim

SULFUR BOTTOM

Indigo dye is applied after sulfur dye; this helps reduce the amount of indigo for darker tones.

The color is similar to indigo denim; it usually produces gray- or yellow-cast denim.

The denim appears more tinted after each wash, often taking on a yellow or gray cast once the indigo layer is washed away.

Blue denim

REACTIVE

The most popular dyestuff for garment dyeing.

Reactive dye produces saturated and consistent color in a wide range of hues.

The denim is unchanged, with excellent color-fastness.

Non-fade denim, colored denim

DENIM SWATCH CARDS

Fiber content
see *Page 060*

Weaving structure of
denim, including yarn size
of both weft and warp

For denim finishing, such
as Mercerization, printing
and coating, see *Page 062*

Raw denim before
washing; usually, mills
only sell raw denim.

For further information about
raw denim, see *Page 046*

DENIM FABRIC

FABRIC CODE FY01234
CONTENT .... 100% cotton
CONSTRUCTION .... 77x46 / 10x10+450D

FINISHING ....
01 BEFORE WASH (RAW)   02 RINSE

Denim mills usually provide buyers with swatch cards. They demonstrate the characteristics of their denim: texture, hand-feel, quality, and different indigo hues after washing. Small swatches are attached to a card that's easy to compare and keep.

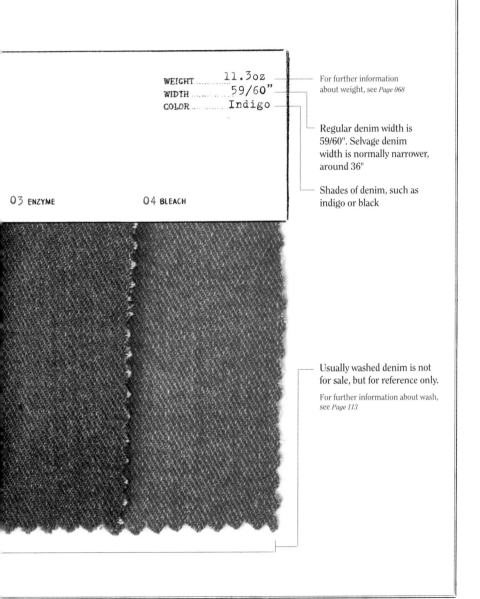

WEIGHT 11.3oz
WIDTH .... 59/60"
COLOR .... Indigo

For further information about weight, see *Page 068*

Regular denim width is 59/60". Selvage denim width is normally narrower, around 36"

Shades of denim, such as indigo or black

03 ENZYME   04 BLEACH

Usually washed denim is not for sale, but for reference only.

For further information about wash, see *Page 113*

RAW DENIM

Also called dry denim, the term refers to unwashed or untreated denim that is rigid and durable. There are 2 types of raw denim: Sanforized and Unsanforized.

ORIGIN

Before the 1960s, denim was primarily a workwear fabric, and mostly raw. In the 1970s, large denim companies start selling washed jeans, saving customers the effort of breaking them in.

SANFORIZED

Sanforized denim is stretched, shrunk and fixed at the mill to help prevent further shrinkage. Jeans made from Sanforized denim are truer in size, making it easy for customers to find the perfect fit.

UNSANFORIZED

Also known as "loomstate" or "shrink-to-fit" denim, it shrinks as much as 10% after the first wash. Some people prefer to shrink their own denim for a personalized fit.

THE CULTURE ᴏꜰ RAW DENIM

Many denim enthusiasts love raw denim, as it is the purest form of the fabric. Raw denim also fades naturally over time, and conforms to the shape of the wearer's body.

Fig. 1. Original

Fig. 2. Worn for 30 months

HERITAGE ART

Denim enthusiasts love the history behind raw denim; in the early days of denim, it was not washed. Today, collecting vintage denim as a treasure is a hobby.

HIGH-CONTRAST FADES

When raw denim is abraded, high-contrast fading can be achieved; the contrast becomes softer with washing.

The wearer can control the level of fading via the amount of laundering and abrasion the jeans receive.

PASSION FOR PERSONALIZATION

The longer raw denim is worn, the more crease marks and patterns are created, and these change according to the wearer's body and lifestyle.

Fig. 3. Phone Marks

SUSTAINABILITY

No washing process is applied to raw denim; this saves a lot of water, chemicals, stones and electricity.

SELVAGE DENIM

Selvage denim refers to the natural edge produced on woven fabric during manufacture to prevent it from unraveling. The denim has colored edges on both the left and right sides. The selvage edge is stronger; 3×1 is the most common weave for selvage denim.

ORIGIN

Before the late 1800s, fabrics such as denim were made by shuttle looms. The manufacturer would weave the fabric all the way to the edges to minimize waste; this was called "self-edge." As technology progressed, projectile looms produced denim at a faster rate and on a larger scale, eventually overtaking shuttle looms.

THE CHARACTERISTICS <u>OF</u> SELVAGE DENIM

COLORED EDGE

Traditional selvage was red and white. Today selvages come in many types and colors. The purpose of selvage color has changed; whereas it once was a way to tell fabrics apart, now it's a brand trademark.

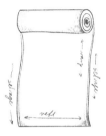

SELF-FINISHED ON BOTH SIDES

Selvage denim is produced by vintage shuttle looms, in which a horizontal weft thread passes through vertical warp threads. The weft thread is continuously passed back and forth, creating a self-finished edge (selvage) so the fabric won't unravel. Other types of loom, including the projectile loom, do not produce selvages.

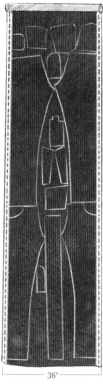

Fig. 2. The pattern for a pair of jeans drawn on a length of selvage denim.

36"

LOWER PRODUCTIVITY AND LESS WIDTH

Producing selvage denim is slower than producing projectile loom-made denim; for one thing, the fabric produced by shuttle looms is only half as wide – typically 36 inches or less.

PREMIUM FEATURE

Selvage denim is rare and slow to produce, making it an expensive choice; hence, it is a sign of premium denim.

For further details about premium denim — *see Page 104*

IS SELVAGE DENIM BETTER THAN OTHER TYPES OF DENIM?

Selvage denim is not necessarily of higher quality than regular denim. The quality of denim depends on the fibers, yarns and even dyes used. However, some people believe that selvage denim fades better, as old shuttle looms weave more slowly, with less yarn tension, and produce more slubs.

BASIC TWILL WEAVE <u>VS.</u> DENIM TWILL WEAVE

BASIC TWILL WEAVE		DENIM TWILL WEAVE
Mostly finer yarn Can be wool, cotton, or a blend	**Yarn**	Mostly coarse yarn Usually cotton
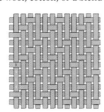	**Diagram**	
Weft yarns pass over 1 warp yarn and under 2 or 3 warp yarns.		White weft yarns pass over 1 indigo warp yarn and under 2 or 3 indigo warp yarns.
Both warp and weft yarns are white, or dyed black/colored.	**Color**	Only the warp yarns are dyed indigo; the weft yarns are white.
Lighter	**Weight**	Heavier
Softer (Desized)	**Hand feel**	Stiffer (Not desized)
Piece dyed according to design and quality.	**Dye method**	Yarn dyed; in denim, only warp yarns are colored. Indigo is not stable enough to for piece-dyeing.
Chinos	**Application**	Jeans

TWILL-WEAVE DENIM

Traditional denim is a cotton twill in which diagonal ribs (also called wales, or twill lines) appear. There are different types of twill denim available.

RHT DENIM RIGHT-HAND TWILL DENIM		**LHT DENIM** LEFT-HAND TWILL DENIM
Woven with S-twist yarn (spun counterclockwise)	**Yarn**	Woven with Z-twist yarn (spun clockwise)
Most common denim direction. Flatter and smoother surface.	**Characteristic**	Softer than RHT denim.
RHT is also called Z-twill	**Direction**	LHT is also called S-twill
The wale runs diagonally from the upper right to the lower left.		The wale runs diagonally from the upper left to the lower right.

TWILL-WEAVE DENIM

	3 X 1 TWILL WEAVE	**2 X 1 TWILL WEAVE**
Characteristic	· Distinct wales · Sturdiest · Most common construction	· Thin and narrow wales · Lighter than 3 x 1 denim · Commonly used for summer
Weaving structure	Three warp yarns for each weft yarn	Two warp yarns for each weft yarn

Warp (Vertical)   Warp (Vertical)

Weft (horizontal)

Warp (Vertical)   Warp (Vertical)

Weft (horizontal)

TWILL-WEAVE DENIM

CAVALRY DENIM	BROKEN TWILL DENIM	HERRINGBONE DENIM
· Protruding twill lines	· Zigzag pattern	· The V-shaped pattern resembles the skeleton of a herring.
Firm warp-faced fabric with a double twill line separated by pronounced grooves formed by the weft.	The weave is reversed every two warp ends to form the unique pattern.	The twill warp stripes are created by running twills in different directions.

STORY

Cavalry twill got its name because it was often used for riding breeches for the British cavalry.

Broken-twill denim was first used by Wrangler in 1964 as a way to reduce the natural torque characteristic of twill weaves, so jeans legs would not twist after washing.

Herringbone weave is named after the skeleton of a herring, whose bones form a zigzag pattern.

NON-TRADITIONAL DENIM

In addition to twill, manufacturers have developed different weave structures for denim.
Today, fabric dyed with indigo is also called denim.

PLAIN WEAVE

	CHAMBRAY	CANVAS DENIM
Characteristic	· Crisscross pattern · often used for work shirts	· Yarns are tightly woven
Weaving structure	Plain weave: each colored warp thread goes over, then under, each white weft thread.	Plain weave: each colored warp thread goes over, then under, each white weft thread.

STORY

The Chambray work shirt is widely known for its use by the U.S. Navy from 1901 to World War II.

Canvas comes in two types: plain and duck. Duck is thicker, heavier and more tightly woven than standard canvas.

SATEEN DENIM	**JACQUARD DENIM**	**KNIT-LIKE DENIM**
· Silky and lustrous fabric made using a satin weave	· Bespoke patterns or designs created on a jacquard loom	· Back is filled with cotton loops, like French terry · Known for its elasticity, softness, comfort and warmth.
4 or more weft threads pass over one warp thread (or vice versa).	Holed punch cards enable the raising and lowering of warp threads to produce complex patterns.	Combines dobby weave and double face.
Satin refers to fabric woven from filament fibers in a satin weave; sateen uses the same weave but is made from short-staple spun yarns.	Jacquard weaving has its origins in sixth-century Italian brocade. It can be created from any material, such as linen and cotton blends.	

DENIM VARIATIONS

Various types of twill denim are developed and classified by color, fiber and yarn characteristics that result in different textures and looks.

	SLUB DENIM	CROSSHATCH DENIM
Yarn	Slub or uneven yarn (irregular thickness)	Slub or uneven yarn
Usage	Warp only	Warp and weft
Appearance	· More textured vertical lines · Produces a vertical fading effect called "vertical falls" (*tate-ochi* in Japanese)	· More of a grid pattern · Produces a crisscross effect as it fades

	NEP DENIM	METALLIC DENIM
Yarn	"Neppy" yarn (full of small knots and broken fibers)	Metallic yarn
Common application	Weft only	Weft only
Appearance	· Looks snowy and furry, with cotton tufts protruding through the surface of the fabric	· Sparkly and luxurious look · Produces shiny metallic flecks

COLOR

ECRU DENIM

Undyed denim retains
cotton's natural hue.

STORY

Coarse twill ecru denim is
called "bull denim."

WHITE DENIM

Denim woven from
bleached cotton.

BLACK DENIM

Warp yarn is dyed with black
sulfur; the weft remains white.

"Black-black" denim means
both sides of the fabric are
black; this can be achieved by
overdyeing or yarn-dyeing.

COLOR

COLORED DENIM

Warp yarn are dyed with reactive or sulfur dyes; the weft remains white. Non-fading colored denim is usually produced by reactive dyes.

> During the 20th century, a wide range of colours has become available, including black, white, red and brown.

COLORED WEFT DENIM

Weft yarns are colored, while the warp yarns are indigo blue.

The face of the denim has thin colored lines between fatter lines of indigo.

FIBER CONTENT

COTTON	FLAX (LINEN)	HEMP

COTTON

Cotton is the most popular fiber for denim. Long-fiber cotton produces better-quality denim.

· Soft
· Breathable
· High tensile strength
· Absorbent
· Shrinks easily
· Highly flammable and burns quickly

FLAX (LINEN)

Flax is used to make "linen denim," which is lightweight, and therefore popular for summer. It is usually used for weft yarn.

· Strong
· Lustrous
· Insect-resistant
· Breathable
· Cool to the touch
· Wrinkles easily

HEMP

A more sustainable choice, hemp shares certain characteristics with linen, but is stronger than linen.

· Super-strong
· Durable
· Breathable
· Anti-microbial
· Cool to the touch
· Wrinkles easily

FIBER CONTENT

ELASTANE (SPANDEX)

A bit of elastane blended with cotton or cotton/polyester results in a softer, stretchier denim.

· Stretchy
· Higher elongation
· Lightweight
· Resists perspiration
· Less breathable
· Heat sensitive

POLYESTER

often blended with natural fibers, polyester helps reduce costs. It is usually used for weft yarn.

· Lightweight
· Durable
· Stretchy
· Quick-drying
· Wrinkles resistant
· Less breathable

RAYON

Rayon is sometimes blended with cotton to enhance draping, especially for shirts.

· Silky soft
· Shiny
· Drapes well
· Easy to dye
· Shrinks when washed

DENIM FINISHING

REGULAR FINISHING

Most denim, including raw denim, undergoes finishing.
It's the last stage of denim production, and is an important factor in the fabric's
performance, appearance and value.

PERFORMANCE

SANFORIZATION (PRE-SHRINKING)

Eliminates shrinkage: Solves a key problem of unfinished denim, and keeps its shape and size stable.

PRE-SKEWING

Eliminates leg twist: Prevents denim from skewing in the direction of the twill line due to washing and shrinking.

HEAT SETTING

Controls stretch: Controls the elasticity and dimensional stability of stretch denim made with thermoplastic fibers such as polyester or elastane.

APPEARANCE

SINGEING

Removes fluff from the fabric's surface: Burns away loose, hairy cotton fibers on the surface of denim, for a smoother feel.

MERCERIZATION

Increases smoothness and luster: The fabric is soaked in a chemical solution that swells the cell walls of the fibers for a more even look and smoother hand feel.

FUNCTIONAL FINISHING

Denim is becoming more functional thanks to the application of new treatments that enhance its performance.

WATER REPELLENT

Water does not penetrate easily, but the fabric remains breathable. There are different levels of water protection: water-resistant, water-repellent and waterproof.

ANTIBACTERIAL

Protects denim from microorganisms including bacteria, mildew, and the deterioration and odors they may cause.

STAIN RESISTANT

Prevents liquids, oils and dirt particles from being absorbed by the fabric.

UV PROTECTION

Absorbs short-wave solar radiation or scatters ultraviolet rays, thereby reducing skin's exposure to ultraviolet rays.

MOSQUITO REPELLENT

This finish emits odors that repel mosquitoes to prevent bites and the viral infections they may transmit.

DENIM COATINGS

Coatings are generally paste and liquid foams made by using pigments, polyurethane or wax coatings or other substances. Coatings can be applied one or more times, and the number of applications may affect appearance and hand feel.

PU COATING
Gives the fabric luster and a rubbery feel; it's also water-resistant.

WAX COATING
There are 2 types of wax: paraffin and beeswax. Paraffin usually has a matte look. Both provide water-resistance.

METALLIC COATING
Provides a shiny surface, and comes in different colors and densities.

Before reflection

After reflection

REFLECTIVE COATING	GLITTER COATING	PIGMENT COATING
Reflects light, making the wearer more visible in the dark.	Adds sparkle to the fabric, and comes in a variety of types and colors.	Results in a worn effect after every wash due to fading properties. Normally used on colored denim.

DENIM PRINTING

Printing is the process of applying agents such as pigments and dyes to the fabric to achieve patterns or designs.

DISCHARGE PRINTING
An indigo-removing agent is printed onto dyed fabric, leaving a bleached-out pattern.

FOIL PRINTING
Metallic or pigment foil is applied by heat and pressure, resulting in a mirrored effect.

PIGMENT PRINTING

Pigments are printed onto the fabric using a roller, rotary screen, or stencil. The print may fade after washing.

FLOCK PRINTING

Short, finely cut natural or synthetic fibers are applied to the fabric with adhesive.

EMBOSS PRINTING

Images or patterns are pressed into the fabric through heat and pressure. This technique creates a 3D effect.

DENIM WEIGHT

The weight of a finished garment can vary from 3 to 32 ounces per square yard; there is no standard weight. The weight of the fabric helps determine its softness, breathability, durability, and tendency to fade. The lower the weight, the softer and more flexible the fabric.

Most denim brands provide weight information on the back-pocket tag.

OUNCES

Ounces per square yard (usually abbreviated as oz/yd²) is a standard used by the denim industry to categorize fabric by weight.

FACTORS THAT INFLUENCE WEIGHT

YARN THICKNESS
The thicker the yarn, the heavier the denim, and vice versa.

STRUCTURE DENSITY
The higher the density, the more yarns it contains, and the heavier the fabric is.

PRINT, COATING OR FINISHING
If a coating is applied, the weight increases.

FIBER CONTENT
Different fibers have different weights. Generally, polyester is lighter than cotton, so a cotton/polyester blend is lighter than 100% cotton denim.

LIGHTWEIGHT DENIM
<9 OZ.

CHARACTERISTICS
· Lighter
· Softer and more pliable
· Breathable, suitable for hot weather
· Drapes well
· Dries more quickly

MIDWEIGHT DENIM
9-12 OZ.

CHARACTERISTICS
· Comfortable
· Can be worn year-round
· Fades well over time
· Versatile
· Strong and durable

HEAVYWEIGHT DENIM
>12 OZ.

CHARACTERISTICS
· Rigid, more durable
· Warmer
· Fades well over time
· Thickest and most protective
· High abrasion resistance

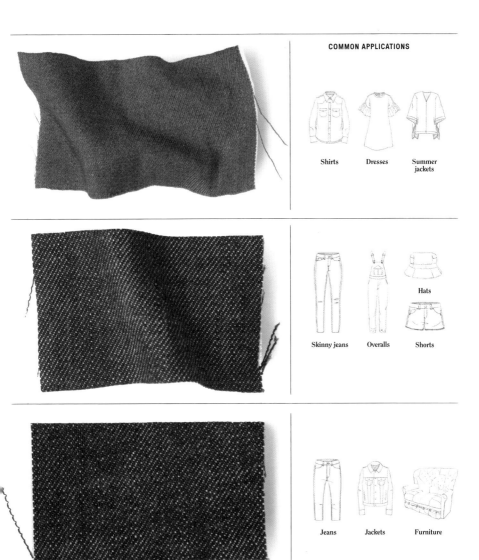

COMMON APPLICATIONS

Shirts   Dresses   Summer
                     jackets

                                Hats

Skinny jeans   Overalls   Shorts

Jeans   Jackets   Furniture

DENIM
Design
FROM FUNCTIONAL
TO FASHIONABLE

The first pair of jeans were called "waist
overalls." In the 1870s, the design of jeans
was practical due the nature of workers' lives
as well as economic and social movements.
However, over the decades, jeans have
evolved from rugged workwear to fashion
staple. There are even designs that change
the shape of the wearer's body. In addition,
rivets and other embellishments have
developed in a variety of colors and styles.

1873

THE ORIGINAL: WAIST OVERALLS

Levi Strauss and Jacob Davis patent and mass
produce "waist overalls." They're held up with
suspenders.
Key front features: A watch pocket, suspender
buttons, a button fly and a rivet in the crotch.
Key back features: A cinch, suspender buttons and
1 pocket with rivets.

THE EVOLUTION
ᴼᶠ BLUE JEANS

Jeans made 100 years ago looked very
different from those made today. Over the
decades, important moments in history
have affected the appearance of jeans, and
they have become more comfortable as a
result of design improvements.

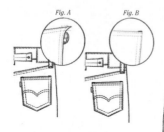

Fig. A   *Fig. B*

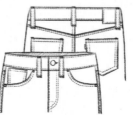

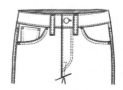

1937

Fig. A BACK POCKET
RIVETS ARE HIDDEN

Because of complaints that copper rivets
scratched saddles and furniture,
Levi Strauss conceals them with fabric.

Fig. B BAR TACKS REPLACE RIVETS

Hidden bar tacks soon replace
hidden rivets.

1942

WWII RATIONING
ALLOWS ONLY BELT LOOPS

During WWII, the U.S. government
requires clothing manufacturers to
conserve materials.

Levi Strauss removes cinches and
the rivets on watch pockets. Only belt
loops remain.

1947

RIVETS RETURN

Rivets are put back on watch pockets.

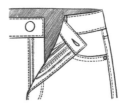

1901

LEFT BACK POCKETS ARE ADDED

Left back pockets are introduced by American brand Levi Strauss.

RENAMED OVERALLS

Waist overalls are now called overalls.

1922

BELT LOOPS ARE ADDED

Belt loops are added, but suspender buttons and the cinch are kept too, allowing customers to choose how they wear their Levi's.

Some customers cut off the cinch and suspender buttons so they can wear a belt, while others keep using the original features.

1926

ZIPPER FLY IS ADDED

The first zip-fly jeans, model 101Z, are introduced to the market by American brand Lee.

1950s

RENAMED JEANS

Teenagers begin using the word "jeans" instead of "overalls." By 1960, the term is being used by manufacturers in ads and on packaging.

1966

BAR TACKS REPLACE RIVETS

Levi Strauss replaces rivets with bar tacks on back pockets.

PRESENT

5-POCKET JEANS LEAD

5-pocket jeans are the most popular denim style, becoming the industry standard.

Key front features: Watch pocket, belt loops, rivets and zipper fly.
Key back features: Belt loops and 2 pockets

CLASSIC DENIM

In the 19th and 20th centuries, denim clothing was originally designed for the working classes. The styles tended to be practical, with details such as hammer loops and tool pockets. These styles are now considered iconic.

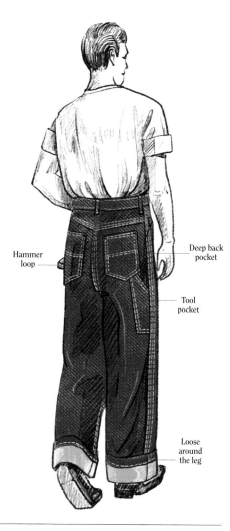

Hammer loop

Deep back pocket

Tool pocket

Loose around the leg

CLASSIC 5-POCKET JEANS

The original waist overalls produced by Levi Strauss in 1873 only had four pockets.

In 1901, a left rear pocket was added. Five pockets are now the industry standard.

CARPENTER JEANS

Carpenter jeans were introduced to the United States from French workwear, and were designed to carry an assortment of tools. They became popular among hip-hop artists in the late 90s and early 2000s.

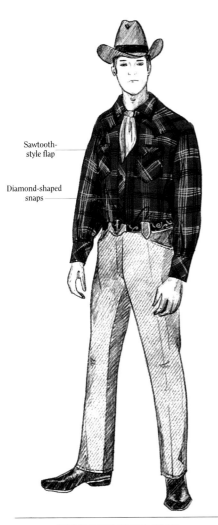

Sawtooth-
style flap

Diamond-shaped
snaps

SAWTOOTH WESTERN SHIRT

The sawtooth Western shirt was created by Jack
Weil, the founder of Rockmount Ranch Wear. He
patented the sawtooth style, and produced the first
Western shirts with snaps in 1946. The Rockmount
sawtooth style with snaps is considered the longest
continuously made shirt in America.

CHAMBRAY WORK SHIRT

The origins of Chambray go back to France in the
1500s. The Chambray work shirt is widely known for
its use by the U.S. Navy from 1901 to World War II,
when it was part of the workwear uniform. The phrase
"blue collar" derives from the shirt, a "blue-collar" job
being one that involves manual labor.

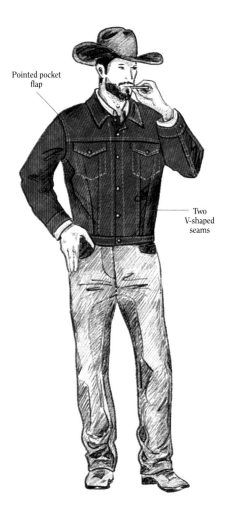

Pointed pocket
flap

Two
V-shaped
seams

TRUCKER JACKET

Levi's Type III jacket (design 557XX),
also known as the Trucker jacket, was
introduced by the brand in 1961 and is
its most popular style. It was the first
jacket with pointed pocket flaps and two
V-shaped seams.

BIB OVERALLS

Lee started manufacturing bib overalls,
originally called "slops," in 1911. During the
Great Depression, farmers wore them as a
symbol to protest the rising cost of clothing and
profiteering in the garment industry. Like other
workwear staples, overalls became fashionable
among hippies in the 1960s.

CHORE COAT

Chore coats emerged in 19th-century France. They were called *bleus de travail* ("worker's blues"). Worn by farmers and manual laborers, the coats were traditionally made from dark blue cotton drill or moleskin that hid dirt. The style is loose-fitting and features 3 or 4 roomy pockets (one of which is a breast pocket). By the 1920s, chore coats were being made all over Europe and the United States, and tended to be denim.

RAILROAD JACKET

Similar to a chore coat, the railroad jacket also came to the United States via France. Carhartt introduced a denim version in 1917 that was known as the "engineer sack coat." It was also called a railroad jacket because many railroad workers wore it.

The jacket is loose fitting, and has 4 or 5 roomy pockets, a pencil pocket on the left side of the chest as well as pocket-watch storage, cuffed sleeves, and ring-back buttons.

CONTEMPORARY DENIM

Since the middle of the 20th century, with the influence of the counterculture and advances in technology, denim clothing has become more fashionable, creative and functional. Today's designs are very adaptable; denim clothing can be lined for cold weather, alter the wearer's body shape, and accommodate certain physical needs, including pregnancy and disabilities.

$\langle$ AESTHETIC $\rangle$

PAINT-SPLATTERED　　　　　　　**CONTRAST STITCHING**

MIXED FABRICS

TWO-TONE

COLOR-BLOCK

EMBELLISHMENT

Studs, embroidered patches, fringe,
metal chains, rhinestones

LAYERING

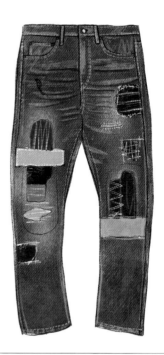

DECONSTRUCTION / REWORKED   **PATCHWORK**

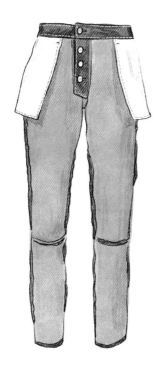

INSIDE OUT   **CUTOUTS**   **ALL-OVER PRINT**
Graphics, logos, text

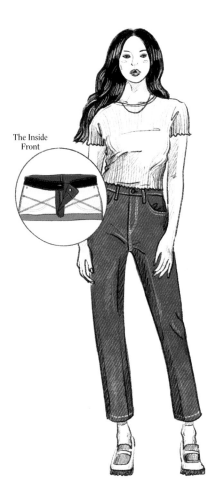

The Inside Front

Adjustable Butt Pad

TUMMY-CONTROL DESIGN

An additional panel is added on the inside front of the jeans. There are several rows of elastic-thread stitches on the panel; some are horizontal, and others are diagonal.

FUNCTION

Diminishes and flattens the belly.

BUTT-LIFTING DESIGN

A diagonal yoke seam extends in a heart shape at the back. This heart-shaped seam helps enhance curves and makes buttocks look naturally rounder and fuller. There's also an adjustable butt pad inside the back panel; this additional function increases the lifting effect.

FUNCTION

Enhances the shape and curve of the buttocks.

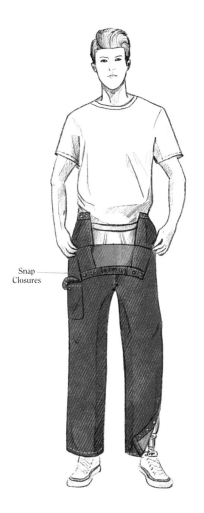

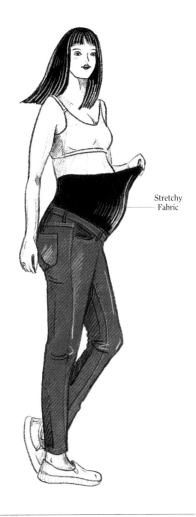

Snap
Closures

Stretchy
Fabric

ADAPTIVE DESIGNS

Adaptive garments have special closures and
design details – including elastic waistbands,
inner waistband loops, Velcro closures and side
zippers – that make them easier for people with
disabilities to use.

These clothes often have a high back rise,
longer legs, and no back pockets or rivets.

FUNCTION

Easy to use, comfortable and multifunctional.

MATERNITY DESIGNS

Instead of a waistband, button or zipper closure,
maternity jeans have a soft, stretchy band of
fabric that encircles the waist and comfortably
accommodates the growing belly.

FUNCTION

Supports the belly as a low-compression girdle,
and provides comfort and ease of movement.

SILHOUETTES

There are many different jeans silhouettes that vary in hem, rise, fit and leg shapes.

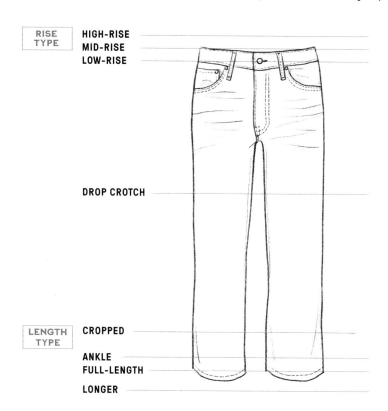

RISE TYPE

HIGH-RISE
MID-RISE
LOW-RISE

DROP CROTCH

LENGTH TYPE

CROPPED

ANKLE
FULL-LENGTH

LONGER

FIT/LEG TYPE

STRAIGHT

SLIM

TAPERED

SKINNY

SUPER-SKINNY

BOOT-CUT

FLARES

BOYFRIEND

MOM

DAD

RELAXED

LOOSE

WIDE-LEG

BAGGY

DESIGN COMPONENTS AND TRIMMINGS

Design elements are a major feature of denim clothing. Some details – such as bar tacks – are for durability and practicality, while others are aesthetic.

A.

C.

B.

1.

3.

4.

DESIGN COMPONENTS	
1. Front pocket	**3.** Cuff
2. Yoke	**4.** Hem

TRIMMINGS

A. Tack button   **C.** Brand patch
B. Rivets   **D.** Buckles

DESIGN COMPONENTS AND TRIMMINGS / JEANS

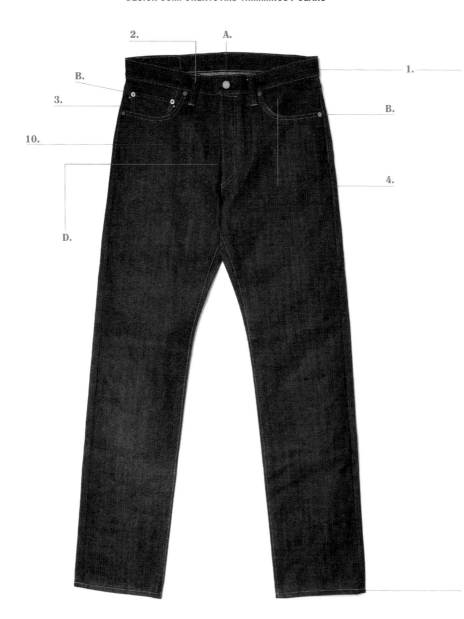

DESIGN COMPONENTS

1. Waistband	**3.** Coin pocket	**5.** Yoke	**7.** Arcuates	**9.** Bar tack
2. Belt loop	**4.** Front pocket	**6.** Back pocket	**8.** Hem	**10.** Fly

9.

C.

5.

6.

7.

FASHIONARY

8.

TRIMMINGS

A. Tack button   **C.** Brand patch
B. Rivets   **D.** Metal zipper

DESIGN LIBRARY
DESIGN COMPONENTS

A quick overview of common design components and
styles in denim clothing, including tops and bottoms.

SHIRTS & JACKETS

FRONT YOKE

The front yoke is a panel that fits around the neck and shoulders, and provides
support for the other pieces of the shirt as well as a decorative element.

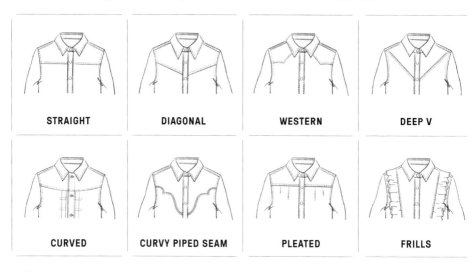

STRAIGHT   DIAGONAL   WESTERN   DEEP V

CURVED   CURVY PIPED SEAM   PLEATED   FRILLS

BACK YOKE

The back yoke is a panel across the back of the shirt that is used to preserve the curve
of the shoulders. Sometimes it provides support for pleats.

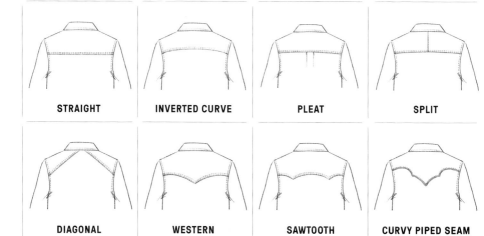

STRAIGHT   INVERTED CURVE   PLEAT   SPLIT

DIAGONAL   WESTERN   SAWTOOTH   CURVY PIPED SEAM

CUFF

The cuff is the fabric at the end of the sleeves; it provides a snug fit around
the wrist and helps prevent fraying.

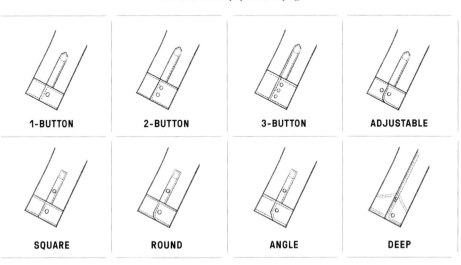

| 1-BUTTON | 2-BUTTON | 3-BUTTON | ADJUSTABLE |

| SQUARE | ROUND | ANGLE | DEEP |

HEM

The hem is the bottom edge of a garment; it is usually folded and sewn to
create a finished edge.

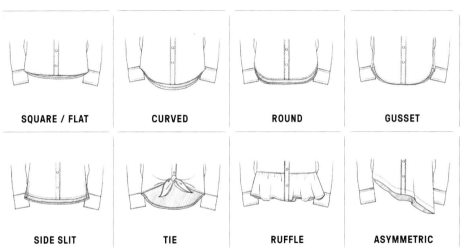

| SQUARE / FLAT | CURVED | ROUND | GUSSET |

| SIDE SLIT | TIE | RUFFLE | ASYMMETRIC |

TRADITIONAL 5-POCKET

There are 2 scoop pockets in the front, a coin pocket inside the right
front pocket, and 2 patch pockets on the back.

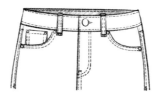

WAISTBAND

A waistband is the piece of fabric at the top of jeans or trousers; often, it is contoured, and made
from fabric that has been cut on the bias. This allows the fabric to move, stretch, and conform to
the shape of the waist for better comfort.

REGULAR   SUSPENDER BUTTONS   WIDE WAISTBAND with double buttons   EXTENDED

ELASTIC   CRISSCROSS   PAPER BAG   DOUBLE WAISTBAND

FLY

Also known as a fly front, the fly conceals the zipper or buttons. The stitching of a zipper on jeans is called
a "J-stitch". Sometimes – for instance, on jeggings – the fly is fake, as there is no fastening to conceal.

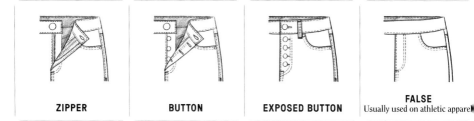

ZIPPER   BUTTON   EXPOSED BUTTON   **FALSE** Usually used on athletic apparel

FRONT POCKET

The front pocket is an inset pocket on both sides of a pair of jeans. It is deeper than
a back patch pocket.

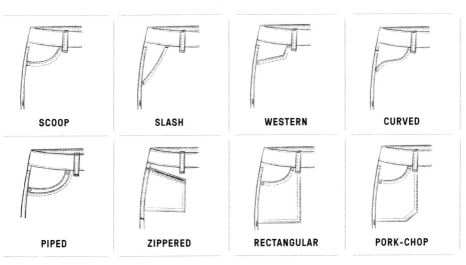

SCOOP	SLASH	WESTERN	CURVED
PIPED	ZIPPERED	RECTANGULAR	PORK-CHOP

COIN POCKET

A small coin pocket, also known as a match pocket, was designed in the 1800s for cowboys'
pocket watches. Nowadays it's handy for coins, tickets and receipts.

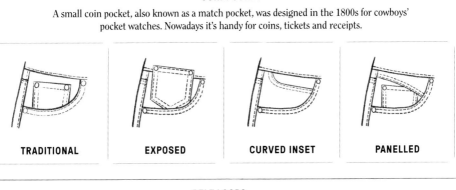

TRADITIONAL	EXPOSED	CURVED INSET	PANELLED

BELT LOOPS

Belt loops are added to the waistband of jeans or trousers, allowing the garment to be worn
with a belt for a better fit. In the past, belt loops were long enough to cover the yoke seam.

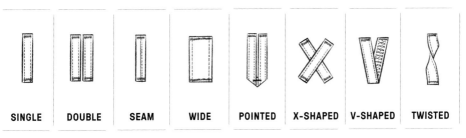

SINGLE	DOUBLE	SEAM	WIDE	POINTED	X-SHAPED	V-SHAPED	TWISTED

BACK YOKE

A yoke can also be called a riser; it is the V-shaped section on the back of jeans.
It facilitates a curved seat and a more fitted waist.

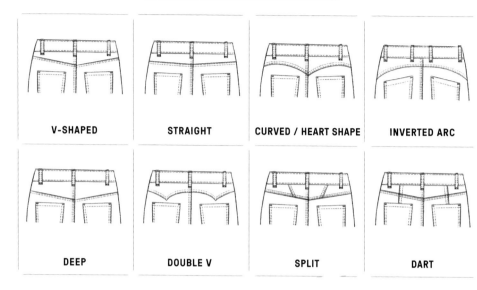

V-SHAPED   STRAIGHT   CURVED / HEART SHAPE   INVERTED ARC

DEEP   DOUBLE V   SPLIT   DART

BACK CINCH

Before belts became popular, the back cinch (with buckle) was a common way to tighten the waist of a pair of jeans. It is usually placed on the back yoke or waistband of jeans, and on the lower back of jackets.

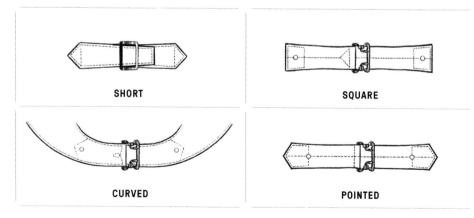

SHORT   SQUARE

CURVED   POINTED

ARCUATES (ARCS)

Arcuates, or arcs, are the decorative stitches on the back pockets of jeans.
They're also known as back pocket signatures. In 1943, Levi's registered its
arcuate as a trademark to prevent copying by other denim brands.

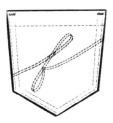

HEM

The hem is the bottom edge of a pair of jeans or trousers. The hem of jeans usually
has more design variations than the hem of shirts and jackets.

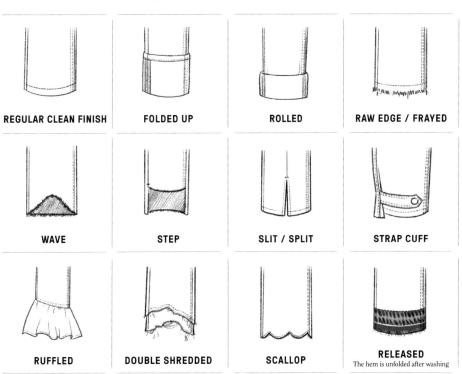

REGULAR CLEAN FINISH | FOLDED UP | ROLLED | RAW EDGE / FRAYED

WAVE | STEP | SLIT / SPLIT | STRAP CUFF

RUFFLED | DOUBLE SHREDDED | SCALLOP | RELEASED
The hem is unfolded after washing

SHIRTS & JACKETS | JEANS & TROUSERS

POCKETS

Pockets are usually placed on the front of shirts and jackets and the back of jeans; they're useful for carrying small items such as wallets and phones. There are 3 main pocket types: patch, inset and in-seam.

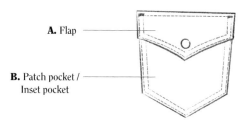

A. Flap

B. Patch pocket / Inset pocket

ANATOMY OF A FLAP POCKET

A flap pocket has a flap over the opening. The flap is sewn on the outside of the garment to keep the contents of the pocket safe.

A. FLAP STYLES

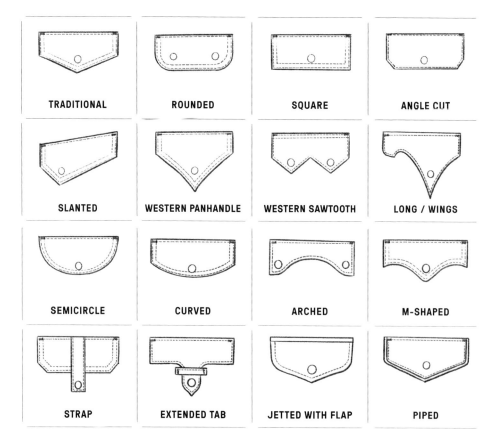

TRADITIONAL

ROUNDED

SQUARE

ANGLE CUT

SLANTED

WESTERN PANHANDLE

WESTERN SAWTOOTH

LONG / WINGS

SEMICIRCLE

CURVED

ARCHED

M-SHAPED

STRAP

EXTENDED TAB

JETTED WITH FLAP

PIPED

PATCH POCKET
Pocket is sewn to the outside of the garment.

INSET POCKET
Only the opening is visible on the outside of the garment; the pocket itself is inside.

IN-SEAM POCKET
The pocket opening falls on the seam line, and the pocket itself is inside the garment.

B. POCKET STYLES

 **POINTED** Traditional

 ROUNDED

 SQUARE

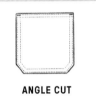 **ANGLE CUT**

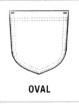 **OVAL**

 **U-SHAPED**

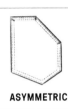 **ASYMMETRIC**

 **CUT SEAM**

 INVERTED PLEAT

 BOX PLEAT

 BELLOWS / GUSSET

 **ZIPPERED PATCH**

 HEART-SHAPE

 **NOTCHED**

 **ARCHED**

 **MULTI-POCKET**

 WELT

 JETTED

 SMILE

DESIGN LIBRARY
TRIMMINGS

ANATOMY OF A TACK BUTTON / RIVET

Button / Rivet head

Fabric

Button / Rivet tack

TACK BUTTON (SHANK BUTTON)

Tack buttons are made from sturdy metal and are used on thick fabric. They are usually used on the front closure of a denim jacket, or the waistband or fly on a pair of jeans. Tack buttons consists of 2 components: the head and the tack.

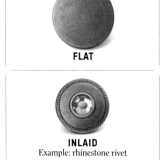

FLAT

DONUT

EMBOSSED

INLAID
Example: rhinestone rivet

SWIVEL BACK
Rotating button

RIVETS

Rivets are used to reinforce the pockets and stress points of denim jeans; they can also be decorative. Rivets consist of 2 components: the head and the tack.

PERFORATED
Classic rivet: copper rivets and burrs

FLAT

NIPPLE

INVERTED NIPPLE

DOMED

INLAID

EMBOSSED

METAL ZIPPER

A zipper is also known as a zip or zip fastener. Unlike plastic zippers, metal zippers do not stretch, so they can take a lot of pressure without breaking or changing shape. They are very durable and able to withstand heavy washing.

CLOSED-END ZIPPER

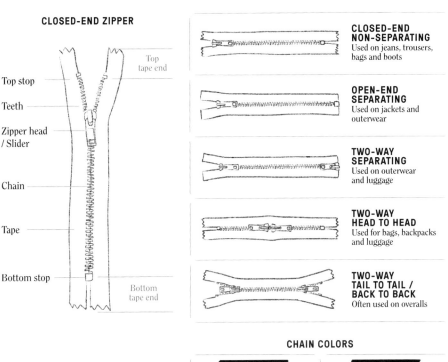

Top
tape end

Top stop

Teeth

Zipper head
/ Slider

Chain

Tape

Bottom stop

Bottom
tape end

**CLOSED-END
NON-SEPARATING**
Used on jeans, trousers,
bags and boots

**OPEN-END
SEPARATING**
Used on jackets and
outerwear

**TWO-WAY
SEPARATING**
Used on outerwear
and luggage

**TWO-WAY
HEAD TO HEAD**
Used for bags, backpacks
and luggage

**TWO-WAY
TAIL TO TAIL /
BACK TO BACK**
Often used on overalls

CHAIN COLORS

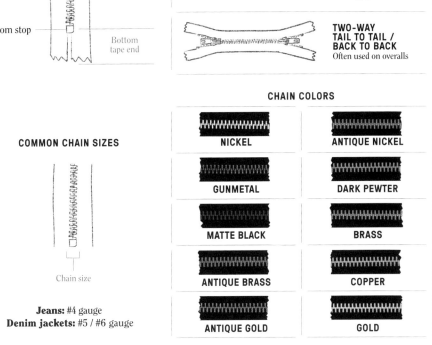

COMMON CHAIN SIZES

Chain size

Jeans: #4 gauge
Denim jackets: #5 / #6 gauge

NICKEL

ANTIQUE NICKEL

GUNMETAL

DARK PEWTER

MATTE BLACK

BRASS

ANTIQUE BRASS

COPPER

ANTIQUE GOLD

GOLD

BAR TACKS

Bar tacks are long, zigzag-like stitches used as reinforcement. The first style of bar tack, called an inner bar tack, is used in place of rivet and is stitched between the edge of the pocket and the surface of the fabric.

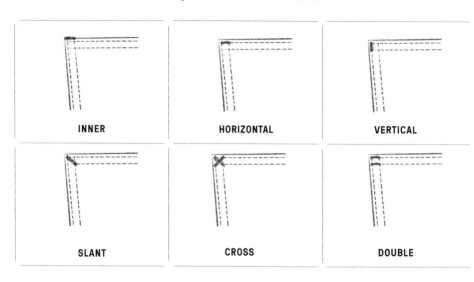

INNER   HORIZONTAL   VERTICAL

SLANT   CROSS   DOUBLE

BUCKLES

The buckle or clasp on a back cinch fastens two loose ends of fabric, allowing the waist of a pair of jeans (or a jacket) to be tightened and loosened.

SLIDING BAR ADJUSTER   RECTANGLE SINGLE PRONG   BENDED WIRE DOUBLE PRONG

DOUBLE SLIDING BAR ADJUSTER   CLASSIC DOUBLE PRONG   COPPER CORE ADJUSTER

THREAD

Thread usage, color, thickness, style, and the number of stitches per inch can all affect the final appearance and function of denim clothing. Designers also use different types of thread to create unique features on their jeans.

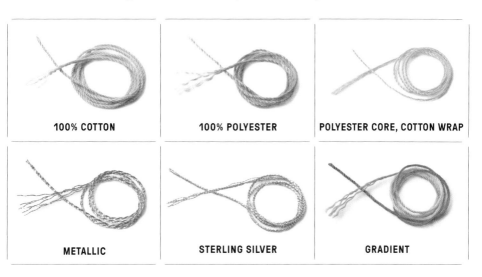

100% COTTON	100% POLYESTER	POLYESTER CORE, COTTON WRAP
METALLIC	STERLING SILVER	GRADIENT

STITCH PER INCH (SPI)

SPI refer to number of stitches in a 1-inch row of sewing.
In the 1920s, most brands used 12–16 SPI. Nowadays, denim garments generally use 7–9 SPI.

7 SPI

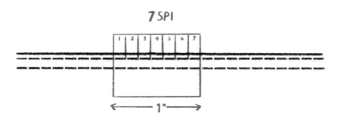

ROWS OF STITCHING

SINGLE STITCH	DOUBLE STITCH	TRIPLE STITCH

BRAND PATCHES

Leather back patches are used for brand recognition; they allow consumers to immediately identify a brand. The patches are also an effective way to prevent counterfeit jeans.

Material **ANIMAL HIDE**
Logo **METALLIC EMBROIDERY**

Material **COTTON CANVAS**
Logo **EMBROIDERY**

Material **MICROFIBER**
Logo **HOT-STAMPED + SCREEN-PRINTED**

Material **RECYCLED PAPER**
Logo **SCREEN-PRINTED**

Material **LEATHER**
Logo **DEBOSSED + SANDED**

Material **SILICON**
Logo **EMBOSSED**

Material **VELCRO LOOP**
Logo **HOT-STAMPED**

Material **REFLECTIVE PU**
Logo **SCREEN PRINTED (BLACK) + STAMPED**

Material **PU**
Logo **HIGH-DENSITY DOT-PRINTED**

Material **THERMOPLASTIC POLYURETHANE (TPU)**
Logo **EMBOSSED + MARBLE PRINTED**

FEATURES <u>OF</u> PREMIUM DENIM

To assess a pair of jeans, one should pay attention to the inside of the jeans as well as the outside. Certain details will help the consumer identify the brand and determine the garment's quality.

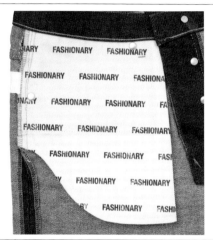

QUALITY POCKET BAGS

Stamped and printed pocket bags usually contain branding and other information. High-quality fabric will strengthen the bag and make it less prone to tearing.

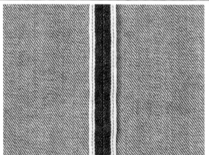

SELVAGE SEAM

A selvage finish can be used in different areas, including coin-pocket edges. If a selvage seam is used on the inside of a garment, it is usually an open seam (as pictured).

CHAIN-STITCHED HEMS

Chain-stitching hems requires a special sewing machine, and is often used on leg openings and waistbands. This stitching method helps increase stretchability and results in better fading patterns, such as a "rope effect," when the jeans are washed.

RAISED BELT LOOPS

Raised belt loops have a 3D appearance because of the central ridge. The ridge is created by the double-folded layer of seam allowance in the middle of the loop.

INNER BAR TACKS

Bar tacks are stitched at the top edge of the back pocket – they're almost invisible.

HIDDEN RIVETS

Hidden rivets are nailed inside the back pocket and covered with fabric on the surface of the garment. The back of the rivet shows on the inside of the garment.

LEFT Outer view / **RIGHT** Inner view

LINED BACK POCKETS

Adding a lining to back pockets increases their durability and helps prevent wear and tear from wallets, keys and the like.

SPECIALIZED SEWING MACHINES
USED <u>IN THE</u> DENIM INDUSTRY

The production of denim garments normally requires the use of heavy-duty sewing machines that can handle thick fabrics. But for some details, other specialized sewing machines are required to achieve a better effect and increase efficiency.

FELLING MACHINE

A felling machine efficiently produces flat felled seams. This type of seam is commonly used on heavy fabric, as it is more durable and refined than overlocking.

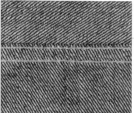

Appearance: Double stitching is visible on the outside; the seam allowance is not visible on the inside (it is enclosed within the seam).

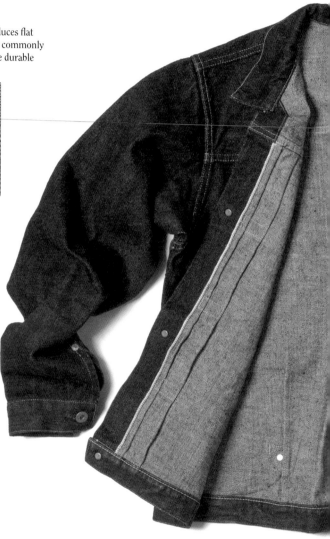

TWIN-NEEDLE MACHINE

A twin-needle machine produces perfectly parallel stitching, called twin or double-needle stitching, on denim garments. 1/4", 5/16" and 1/8" are the most common sizes.

Appearance: Parallel top-stitching.

KEYHOLE MACHINE

A keyhole machine produces keyhole-shaped buttonholes, which can accommodate larger buttons. They are the industry standard, and are recommended for denim garments.

Appearance: Protruding thick chain stitches with a long drop shape.

WAISTBAND MACHINE

A waistband machine folds, sews and attaches the waistband on jeans or jackets with an assist tool.

Appearance: Single stitching on the outside, chain stitching on the inside.

BAR-TACK MACHINE

A bar-tack machine sews bar tacks semi-automatically. Stitch width and length can be adjusted to create different types of bar tacks.

Appearance: Very tight, narrow zigzag stitches.

BELT-LOOP MACHINE

A belt-loop machine folds and sews belt loops with the assistance of folding tool. The twin-needle stitch is the most common style.

Appearance: Twin-needle stitch on the outside, cover stitch on the inside.

HEMMING MACHINE

A hemming machine folds the hem twice and sews with one continuous thread that loops back on itself automatically.
A chain-stitched hem is a traditional look that creates a rope effect after the garment is washed.

Appearance: Single stitching on the outside, chain-stitching on the inside.

CHAPTER 4

The Complete
DENIM
WASH LIBRARY

ESTD | DRY / WET | 1960S

Washing is a vital step in denim processing. Usually done
at the final stage of production, washing changes denim's
appearance and hand feel, which adds value to the clothing.
The process creates different indigo fading effects, which vary
based on the chemicals, conditions, and equipment used.

The experience and workmanship of the laundry's technician
is another factor that affects the final results. Sometimes,
designers will provide reference samples to technicians so
they can see, feel and better understand the desired effect.

PAGE — PAGE
110 — 165

DENIM
WASHING PROCESSES

01
DRY PROCESS
Abrasion treatments
are applied, such as
whiskering and sanding.
For further details — Page 114

02
DESIZING
Sizing agents are
removed from the warp
yarns in woven fabrics.

03
WET PROCESS
Wet processes
include rinsing and
stone washing.
For further details — Page 136

04 *Optional*
BLEACHING
An oxidative bleaching agent
decolorizes the indigo.

05 *Optional*
NEUTRALIZATION
Removes potassium
permanganate (PP)
and hypochlorite residues
from a processed garment.

06 *Optional*
TINTING / DYEING
Add color or create
patterns by tying and
dipping in dye.
For further details — Page 170

07 *Optional*
SOFTENING
Softeners make the
fabric smooth and prevent
static electricity.

08 *Optional*
3D EFFECTS / CURING
A resin solution is applied to
the wrinkle or other effect,
then the garment is fixed in a
curing oven.
For further details — Page 128

WASHING TYPES

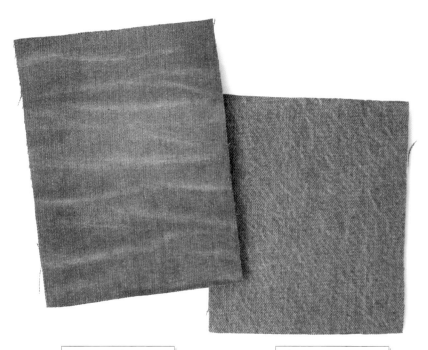

	DRY PROCESS			WET PROCESS
	= DRY FINISHING			= WET FINISHING

DRY PROCESS	Definition	WET PROCESS
The garment is dry; no water is used. It is generally used before wet process.	**Definition**	Liquid chemicals and water are used. Pumice can be added if necessary.
· Creates abrasion · Creates 3D effects · Adds color	**Purpose**	Creates fading (the overall effect will depend on the type and amount of chemicals, the temperature, and the duration).
Parts of the garment	**Areas affected**	Whole garment
· Abrasive tools · Small machines	**Machines / Tools**	Large machines

DRY PROCESS

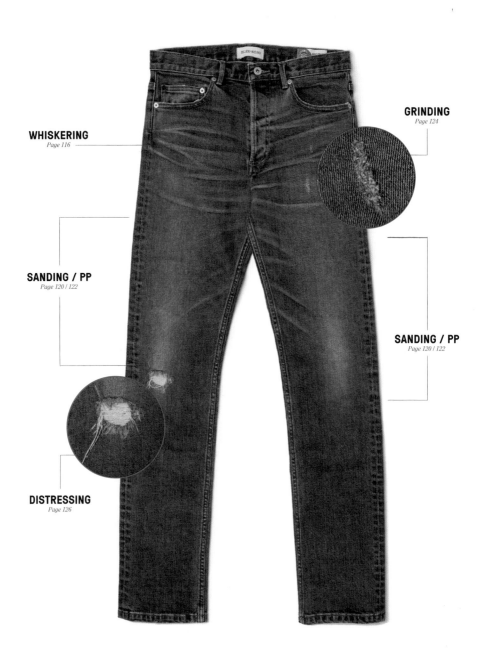

WHISKERING
Page 116

GRINDING
Page 124

SANDING / PP
Page 120 / 122

SANDING / PP
Page 120 / 122

DISTRESSING
Page 126

Dry process is usually done before wet process. The result depends very much on the workmanship, and the quality and effects may not be consistent. The appearance of denim can be changed with abrasion or chemical treatments, and by using small machines and abrasive tools. This process can add value and a unique appearance to denim.

TACKING
Page 118

GRINDING
Page 124

SANDING / PP
Page 120 / 122

GRINDING
Page 124

WHISKERING
Page 116

DISTRESSING
Page 126

PIGMENT SPRAY
Page 132

WHISKERING

Also known as "mustaches" or hige, whiskers are prefabricated patterns that imitate the naturally occurring horizontal creases that form on well-worn jeans. Different strengths and shapes of whiskers imitate different types of wear and tear.

Whiskering

COMMON APPLICATIONS

Front thigh
to crotch

Inner thigh
(aka Chevrons)

Front of knee
(aka Knee stars)

Back of knee
(aka Honeycomb)

EFFECTS

· Additional fading on jeans, especially from the thigh to the crotch.
· Usually tighter, straighter whiskers for skinny jeans, and wider whiskers for looser jeans.

TIPS

· Slightly curved whiskers provide a more natural look.

· Do hand scraping after machine scraping for a softer layering of whiskers.

· Long whiskers should reach, or even pass over, the side seam.

· Do not make whiskers in the patch-pocket area.

PROCESSES

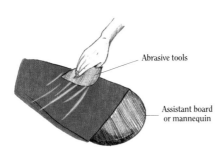

Abrasive tools

Assistant board or mannequin

Whisker pattern block

METHOD 1
HAND SCRAPING

1. Mark the whisker outlines on the jeans.
2. Scrape the surface, following the outlines with abrasive tools.

METHOD 2
WHISKER PATTERN + HAND SCRAPING

1. Insert the whisker pattern block into the jeans.
2. Manually scrape the surface.

TOOLS & MACHINES

Abrasive sandpaper / Sponges

Whisker pattern block

Sandpaper wheel brushing machine

Mannequins (vertical or horizontal)

TACKING

Tacking creates high-contrast fades and 3D effects at specific areas through pleating or folding. It is achieved by holding multiple folds of fabric together with plastic fasteners like those that attach price tags to clothing.

Tacking

COMMON APPLICATIONS

Waistband

Front pocket

Side seam

Back pocket

EFFECTS

· The inside of the folded area is less exposed, so it will remain dark.

· The outside will receive more abrasion, and therefore fade.

TIPS

· Avoid using very fine fasteners, as they may break during washing.

· Pay attention to the needle weight and denim weight; if the needle is too heavy for the fabric, pinholes may occur.

· Do not use thick fasteners on thin denim, or overload the fastener, as doing so will leave pinholes in the fabric.

· Remove the plastic fasteners before drying for a more natural shape and fading effect.

· Alternatively, leave the plastic fasteners on the garment during drying for a higher-contrast effect.

PROCESSES

METHOD 1
MACHINE TACKING
1. Hold the folds together.
2. Using a tagging gun, place the needle through the folds and squeeze the trigger to tack them together.
3. Wash the garment.
4. Remove the plastic fasteners.

METHOD 2
HAND STITCHING
1. Sew the folds shut.
2. Wash the garment.
3. Remove the threads.

TOOLS & MACHINES

Needle and thread

Tagging gun and plastic fasteners

SANDING

Sanding creates natural-looking fading on areas of a garment. The fading level is also affected by the use of coarse or fine sandpaper and other abrasion tools, which produce different effects.

SANDING LEVEL

LIGHT

MEDIUM

HEAVY

Sanding

COMMON APPLICATIONS

Front thigh   Knee   Hip   Yoke

EFFECTS

· The faded area becomes whiter, giving the denim a worn appearance and making its surface smoother.

TIPS

· Coarse abrasive tools are suitable for heavyweight denim, while fine sandpaper is better for lightweight denim.

· Avoid sanding hairy denim, as it will cause pilling.

PROCESSES

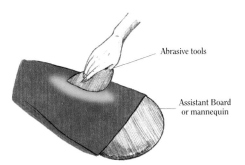

Abrasive tools

Assistant Board or mannequin

Sandblasting is now prohibited in most countries due to health hazards: workers inhale large amounts of silica dust particles generated during the process, which can cause silicosis.

METHOD 1
HAND SCRAPING / HAND SANDING

The surface of the denim is scraped or sanded.

EFFECT
· Natural-looking
· Easy to control the final effect

METHOD 2
SANDBLASTING

Sand or other particles are fired at the garment under high pressure and at high speed.

EFFECT
The fading effect is even dangerous to workers, so the machine needs to be used in isolation.

TOOLS & MACHINES

Abrasive sandpaper / Sponges

Sandblasting machine

Mannequins (vertical or horizontal)

POTASSIUM PERMANGANATE (PP)

Also called monkey wash, PP is a chemical treatment and potent oxidant used to create localized areas of abrasion. PP appears pink on the denim when it's fresh, and turns muddy brown after drying. The denim needs to be washed and treated with hydrogen peroxide to remove the brown manganese oxide.

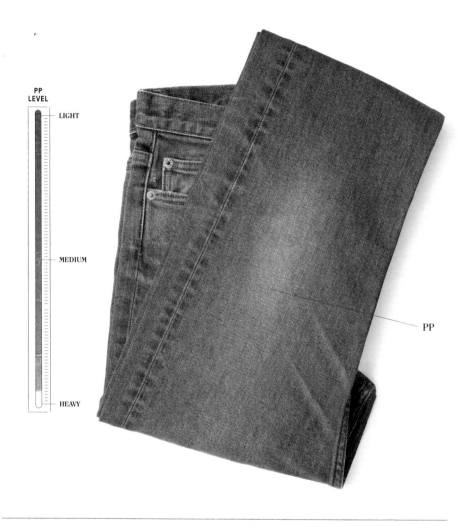

PP LEVEL

- LIGHT
- MEDIUM
- HEAVY

PP

COMMON APPLICATION

Front thigh to knee

Back of knee

Hip

Yoke

EFFECTS

· Produces a worn look on certain areas.

· The center of the sprayed area is whiter, while the edge appears blurry and fades out.

	POTASSIUM PERMANGANATE		HAND SANDING
Substance	Chemical		Sandpaper
Principle	PP solution spray is absorbed into the denim		Direct friction between denim and sandpaper
Effect / Characteristics	· Hard to produce a natural look · Easier to create a white area with less effort · Low friction; less damage to fabric		· Easier to produce a natural look and different layers · Produces a soft effect (depending on coarseness of paper, and pressure used)
Production	Fast		Slow

Best Application: The best effect is produced by using PP for more white areas, then hand sanding to add different levels of fading; this looks prettier and more natural.

PROCESSES

METHOD 1	METHOD 2	METHOD 3
PP SPRAY	**PP RUBBING**	**PP SPOTS**

PP SPRAY
1. Place the garment on the mannequin.
2. Spray PP on the garment using a spray gun.
3. Remove brown oxide with hydrogen peroxide.
4. Neutralize

EFFECT
PP can be evenly spread, creating a softer fade edge.

PP RUBBING
1. Rub PP onto the garment with a towel or sponge.
2. Remove brown oxide with hydrogen peroxide.
3. Neutralize

EFFECT
Creates a stronger contrast, also known as the high-low effect.

PP SPOTS
1. Sprinkle PP onto the garment with a brush.
2. Remove brown oxide with hydrogen peroxide.
3. Neutralize

EFFECT
Creates faded spots that look more natural and whiter than bleach spots.

TOOLS & MACHINES

Mannequins
(vertical or horizontal)

PP spray cabin
(contains spray guns and rubber dummies)

TIPS

· Cover any metal embellishments with tape or fabric when spraying to avoid oxidation or corrosion.

· Place fabric flat without any wrinkles or thread ends before spraying, or the effect will be uneven.

· Neutralize to prevent denim from yellowing.

GRINDING

Grinding wears away denim's surface. The effect is usually
applied to the seams of denim clothing, imitating the worn-out spots
generated by wear and tear.

Grinding

COMMON APPLICATIONS

Pocket edge   Waistband   Hems

EFFECTS

· Small, worn-out white holes.

· The warp yarns are partially damaged,
revealing the white weft yarns.

TIPS

· Apply grinding before washing for a more natural look. The indigo
will lightly stain the white weft yarn.

· Avoid grinding on high-stretch denim, or the grind holes will wrinkle
(the elastic yarn will shrink).

PROCESS

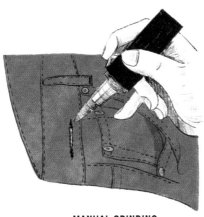

MANUAL GRINDING
Gently touch the surface of the denim with
the grinder until the warp breaks.

TOOLS & MACHINES
The choice of machine will depend on the size,
shape and severity of distressing required.

Micro air grinder   Grinding wheel

DISTRESSING

Distressing, also known as damaging or destroying, imitates the broken-in look of vintage jeans. It is similar to grinding, but the area is larger and there is more damage.

Distressing

TYPES OF DISTRESSING

Ripped

Ripped and Repaired

COMMON APPLICATIONS

Knee   Thigh   Front pocket   Back pocket

EFFECTS

· The warp yarns are damaged, leaving white weft yarns visible in the hole.

· Alternatively, both warp and weft yarns are damaged, leaving an empty hole.

TIPS

· Distress denim before washing for more natural fraying and fringes.

· Avoid distressing high-stretch denim, as the holes will look wrinkled and uneven. The white yarn will curve as the elastic yarn shrinks.

PROCESSES

METHOD 1
HAND DISTRESSING

1. Touch the grinder to the surface of the denim until yarns break.
2. One or both of the yarns can be broken, depending on the effect desired.

METHOD 2
MACHINE DISTRESSING

1. Design the distress effect onto the mold.
2. Put the garment into the distressing machine.
3. Leave until one or both of the yarns are broken.

TOOLS & MACHINES

The choice of machine will depend on the size, shape and severity of distressing required.

Micro air grinder   Grinding wheel   Jeans distressing machine

RESIN APPLICATION

In resin application, a transparent coating creates 3D creases, wrinkles or lines in specific areas.

3D whiskers

Resin coating

COMMON APPLICATIONS

Front thigh
to crotch

Hem

Back of knee

Whole garment

EFFECTS

· The creases and wrinkles fixed by the resin remain stiff, dry and lustrous.

· The resin also reduces pilling.

TIPS

· Do a test patch before applying resin to stretch denim, as it will affect stretchability.

· Inappropriate curing temperature or time will cause the resin to crack.

· If needed, apply PP before resin to avoid an uneven effect.

ECO OPTION

Resin normally contains formaldehyde.

Today there is formaldehyde-free resin that can achieve similar 3D crinkle effects, but it does not work as well as traditional resin.

PROCESSES

METHOD 1
SPOT COVERAGE

1. Spray the resin solution onto small areas.
2. Add creases and wrinkles.
3. Place in the curing oven.

EFFECT
Wrinkles in certain areas: Only parts of the jeans are wrinkled, such as 3D whiskers.

METHOD 2
FULL COVERAGE

1. Place the jeans on the mannequin.
2. Move the mannequin to create creases.
3. Spray the resin solution onto the jeans.
4. Place in the curing oven.

EFFECT
Overall wrinkles: The whole pair of jeans is affected.

METHOD 3
COATING

1. Spray or dip the jeans in resin solution.
2. Place in the curing oven.

EFFECT
No wrinkles: The denim is rigid and has a dry hand feel.

TOOLS & MACHINES

Curing oven

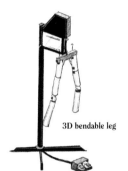

3D bendable leg

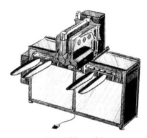

3D crinkle machine (for small areas)

LASER DISTRESSING

Lasers are a more environmentally friendly dry-processing method, as they use no chemicals and much less water.
Different effects can be achieved with lasers, and the quality is more consistent and more efficient for mass production.

EFFECTS
· The indigo surface is burned out and faded.
· The intensity and duration of the laser are key factors that determine the effect.

STORY

The first laser-distressing technology for denim garments was developed by a Florida company, Icon Laser Solutions LLC. The company obtained a patent for the revolutionary denim-finishing method in 1994.

TIPS

· Avoid the use of high-intensity lasers on lightweight denim, as they can burn the fabric.

· Hand-sand after laser-finishing for a more natural effect.

PROCESS

STEP 1
PREPARATION

1. Design the laser pattern.
2. Place the jeans flat inside the laser machine.

STEP 2
LASERING

Lasers burn away the surface of the denim.

STEP 3
WASHING

A final wash cycle removes the fine layer of ash.

LASER APPLICATION		TRADITIONAL WASH
Finer lines can be made. All effects can be achieved.	**Effect**	More natural-looking. More levels of indigo fading.
Less water and fewer chemicals are used.	**Environmental aspects**	More water and chemical waste.
High	**Productivity**	Low
Very consistent	**Consistency**	Inconsistent but unique
More space is required for laser equipment.	**Limitations**	Different washes require different machines.
Higher initial investment costs, uses more electricity.	**Costs**	Lower machine costs, but higher labor costs.

MACHINES

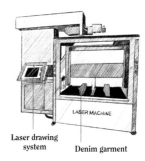

Laser drawing system

LASER MACHINE

Denim garment

PIGMENT SPRAY

Pigment can be applied to certain areas of denim clothing with a spray gun.
The pigment will penetrate the fabric.

PROCESS
Apply the pigment with a
spray gun.

TIPS
Place the garment flat
when spraying, or the effect
will be uneven.

EFFECT
Gives the appearance
of stains.

PIGMENT SPLATTERS

A pigment is splattered across areas of denim clothing with a brush.
The "paint" is mixed with an adhesive binder and will not penetrate the garment, but will stay on the surface instead.

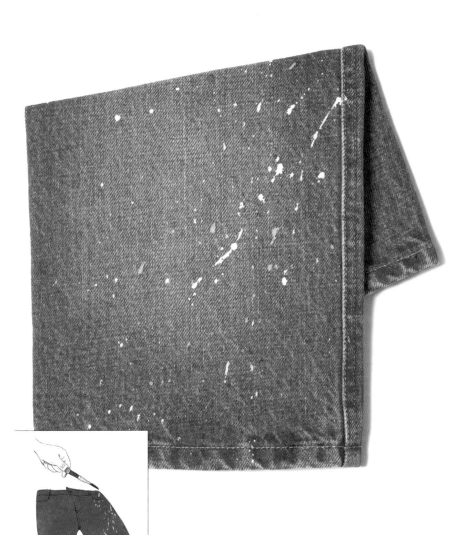

PROCESS
Splatter or paint the pigment onto the denim using a brush.

TIPS
To fix the pigment after application, place the garment in the drying oven.

EFFECT
· Creates an artistic, handcrafted appearance.
· The "paint" provides texture on the surface of the denim.

BLEACH SPOTS

A bleach solution is applied to certain areas of the garment with a brush. It is similar to PP spots, but uses a different chemical. Bleach does more damage to the fabric than PP does.

PROCESS
Splatter the bleach solution with a brush, then neutralize it to prevent yellowing.

TIP
It is best to use potassium permanganate (PP) instead of bleach to reduce damage to the denim.

EFFECT
Small white spots on the denim as the indigo is bleached out.

CREASE MARKS

Faded crease marks are added to certain areas of a denim garment through twisting and tying.

PROCESS
Twist and tie up parts of the denim garment before washing.

TIPS
· The length of a crease mark is related to how the denim is tied.

· The overall look is affected by time, chemicals, and the number of washes.

EFFECT
White crinkle marks will appear after one or more washes.

WET PROCESS

The wet process refers to washing denim along with chemicals or stones, at a certain temperature, according to the formula. During the process, the indigo fades and impurities are removed.

This brings a new look to the garment: it becomes soft, light and unevenly faded through bleaching. The wet process is usually carried out after dry processing, and usually only one or two wet processes are used on a denim garment.

RAW
Page 26

RINSE WASH

Chemical

Page 138

ENZYME WASH

Chemical

Page 139

STONE WASH

Mechanical

Page 140

BLEACH WASH

Chemical

Page 141

CLOUD WASH

Mechanical

Page 144

ICE WASH

Chemical

Page 143

ACID WASH

Chemical

Page 142

RINSE WASH

Also called garment wash, rinse wash is a simple process, and the most common wet-finishing method. It usually contains washing detergent and softener.

WASH
LEVEL

- LIGHT
- MEDIUM
- HEAVY

*SOFTENING
Softeners are used to improve the hand feel of
a garment, making it smooth and preventing
static electricity.

PROCESS	TIPS	EFFECT
1. Desize the garment first, then rinse in 60°C / 140°F water. 2. Wash with detergent, followed by a rinsing and softening* cycle.	Rinse wash can be used intermittently, along with other washing methods. It can be used to lighten the color of the fabric or remove chemical agents.	· Only a little indigo dye will be washed off. · Removes dust and starch from the surface of the denim.

ENZYME WASH

Enzymes are biological catalysts that speed up biochemical reactions and degrade cellulose. Also known as bio stoning, enzyme washing is more environmentally friendly than stone washing.

ENZYME STONEWASH
This term refers to a stone wash applied after an enzyme wash. The finished appearance features random patterns, and creates a soft and fluffy denim.

PROCESS	TIPS	EFFECT
Enzymes eat away the cellulose in the cotton, enhancing fabric-to-fabric abrasion during washing. The indigo dye is also removed, along with surface fibers. A rinsing and softening cycle follows.	Enzyme washing works best with certain temperatures and pH values — usually 50°C to 60°C, either neutral or acidic. Otherwise, its effect will be diminished.	· Fades naturally · Results in soft, fluffy fabric · Removes hairy fibers from the surface

STONE WASH

Stones such as pumice* are added to a hydro extractor (without water) or a paddle washing machine (with water). Stones of different size, shape, hardness and porosity produce different effects.

STORY

François Girbaud, of French brand Marithé + François Girbaud, was the first to industrialize the process of stone washing in the mid-1970s.

In the 1950s, it is said that Donald Freeland, an employee of the Great Western Garment Company, invented the stone washing of denim.

SAND WASH
Developed around 1988, sand wash usually uses smaller pumice stones, and the wash includes alkaline and oxidizing agents. The process creates a marbled look that's lighter than stone wash.

*PUMICE
A lightweight and soft porous stone produced by a volcanic explosion.

PROCESS
In the washing machine, sufficient water must be used to submerge the stones and the garment.

As the washing-machine drum rotates, the stones strike and scrape the fabric repeatedly.

TIPS
· Large, hard stones are more durable, and are suitable for heavier denim.

· Smaller, softer stones work best for lightweight denim, and create delicate patterns.

EFFECT
· Aged appearance

· Random faded patterns and holes

· Seams usually become more faded

BLEACH WASH

A strong oxidative bleaching agent such as chlorine fades or removes the indigo color.

NEUTRALIZATION

An important step, neutralization removes the yellow residue produced by chlorine bleach, leaving a bluer denim. It also helps restore jeans to a neutral pH value (from acidic to alkaline), reducing the risk of skin irritation.

PROCESS

Add a strong oxidative bleaching agent during washing, then neutralize.

The fading level usually depends on the intensity of the bleaching agent, bleach-to-water ratio, temperature and treatment time.

TIPS

· Reactive-dyed colors will change if chlorine bleach is used.

· For even fading, it is important to add the bleaching agent in the same direction as the rotating drum in the washing machine.

EFFECT

· Lightens the denim, or can even turn it completely white.

ACID WASH

Also known as marble wash, moon wash and snow wash.
This process is carried out with pumice stones and a bleach solution in a hydro extractor (without water) or a paddle washing machine (with water). Potassium permanganate (PP) is the most common solution used in acid wash, which is also referred to as PP wash.

STORY

It is said that a night-shift worker forgot to open a water valve while washing jeans, and pumice stones that were damp with a weak bleach solution were accidentally tumbled with the jeans. Later, in 1986, the modern process of acid washing was patented in Italy by the Rifle jeans company.

PROCESS

1. Soak the pumice stones in the bleach solution, then tumble the garment in the hydro extractor or washing machine.

2. Remove the dust and residue with clean water.

3. Lastly, neutralize and apply a softening agent.

TIPS

Sponges, Styrofoam and pumice stones have different levels of abrasiveness, so create different effects.

EFFECT

· Aged, distressed appearance.

· Produces a sharp contrast between blue and white areas.

· The blue area is usually larger than the white area.

ICE WASH

Ice wash is achieved by using more pumice stones combined with a bleach solution such as potassium permanganate; it's like a double acid wash.

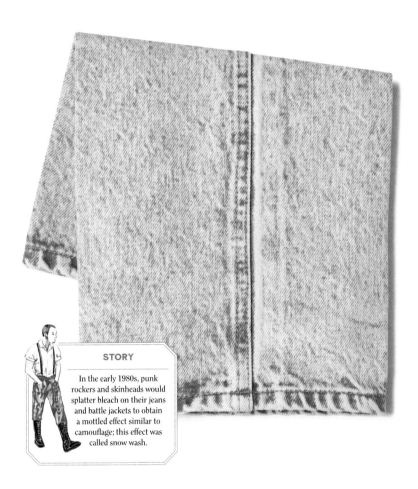

PROCESS

Similar to acid wash, the ice wash process uses more stones and bleach solution, and the garment spends a longer time in the washing machine.

After rinsing, neutralize and apply a softening agent.

EFFECT

· The white area is usually larger than the blue area (the opposite of acid wash).

· Denim is bleached to a light blue color, almost white.

CLOUD WASH

Cloud wash is a kind of acid wash, which is a process carried out with soft abrasive materials and a bleach solution such as potassium permanganate (PP).

	ACID WASH	ICE WASH	CLOUD WASH
Abrasive materials	Pumice stones	More pumice stones than acid wash	Styrofoam
Bleach solution	Added at beginning	Added at beginning	Added little by little
Duration	Short	Long	Long

PROCESS
1. Add PP little by little while the washing machine spins; the PP blends uniformly, along with the soft abrasive materials.

2. After rinsing, neutralize and apply a softening agent.

TIPS
Add more and bigger abrasive materials to increase the friction if only a few garments are in the washing machine.

EFFECT
· Softer and blurrier, with cloud-like patterns.

· An even amount of blue and white; the colors seem to merge.

MACHINES USED ᴵᴺ WET PROCESS

PADDLE WASHING MACHINE

A paddle washing machine can accommodate a wide range of wet processes including washing, bleaching and dyeing.
The garments are moved by a rotating paddle that moves the garment into and out of the water / dye / bleach solution.

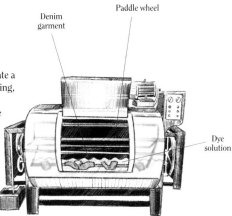

Paddle wheel

Denim garment

Dye solution

HYDRO EXTRACTOR

Also known as a centrifuge, a hydro extractor removes water from clothes after washing. The inner drum rotates at a high speed, forcing the water out.

TUMBLE DRYER

Also known as a steam dryer, a tumble dryer circulates heated air to evaporate the moisture from wet clothing.

Patchwork

PP spraying,
hand sanding

KEY STEPS

01 Dry process Hand sanding	02 Desizing	03 Stone washing	04 Bleach washing	05 Tumble drying
06 Adding patchwork	07 Dry process PP spraying	08 Neutralizing	09 Rinsing	10 Tinting	11 Tumble drying

WASH LIBRARY

SHIRTS / JACKETS / JEANS / SHORTS / SKIRTS

PP spraying
/ rubbing

Grinding

KEY STEPS

01 Dry process Hand sanding	02 Desizing	03 Enzyme stone washing	04 Ozone washing Bleaching	05 Tumble drying
06 Dry process Grinding, PP spraying / rubbing	07 Neutralizing	08 Tinting	09 Tumble drying	10 Pigment spraying	11 Curing

PP spraying

Raw bottom edge

KEY STEPS

01 Dry process Hand sanding, cutting hem	02 Desizing	03 Stone washing	04 Bleach washing	05 Tumble drying
06 Dry process PP spraying	07 Neutralizing	08 Rinsing	09 Tumble drying	10 Tinting	11 Tumble drying

PP rubbing, hand sanding

Grinding

Ripped and repaired

Grinding

Resin

PP rubbing, hand sanding

Bleach spot

KEY STEPS				
01 **Dry process** Hand sanding	02 **Desizing**	03 **Stone washing** Short cycle	04 **Tumble drying**	05 **Dry process** Grinding, PP spraying and rubbing, adding bleach spots
06 **Neutralizing**	07 **Rinsing**	08 **Tumble drying**	09 **Sewing patches** Ripped and repaired areas	10 **Spraying resin on sleeves**	11 **Curing in oven**

PP spraying
/ rubbing

PP spraying/ rubbing,
pigment spray

Paint
splatters

PP spraying
/ rubbing

KEY STEPS

01 Dry process Hand sanding	02 Desizing	03 Stone washing	04 Bleach washing	05 Tumble drying	06 Dry process PP spraying/ rubbing
07 Neutralizing	08 Rinsing	09 Tinting	10 Tumble drying	11 Pigment spraying	12 Adding paint splatters	13 Curing in oven

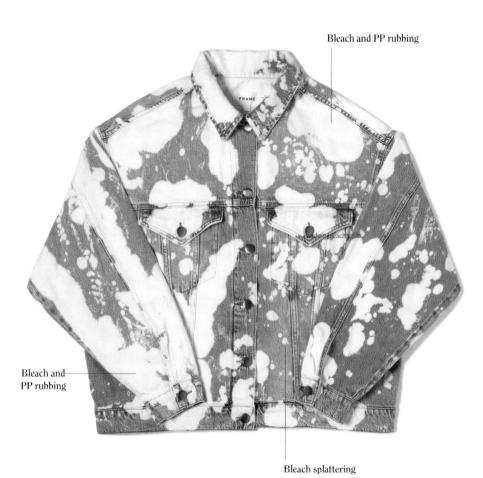

Bleach and PP rubbing

Bleach and
PP rubbing

Bleach splattering

KEY STEPS

01 Dry process Hand sanding	02 Desizing	03 Enzyme stone washing Heavy stones	04 Bleach washing	05 Tumble drying
06 Dry process Grinding, distressing, PP rubbing, adding bleach spots	07 Rubbing bleach and PP solution for big splotches	08 Neutralizing	09 Rinsing	10 Tumble drying

PP spraying,
pigment spraying
(yellow)

PP spraying,
pigment spraying
(darker blue)

PP spraying,
hand sanding

PP spraying,
pigment spraying (yellow)

KEY STEPS

01	02	03	04	05	06
Dry process Hand sanding	Desizing	Enzyme stone washing	Bleach washing	Tumble drying	Dry process PP spraying
07	08	09	10	11	12
Neutralizing	Rinsing	Tumble drying	Pigment spraying	Rinsing	Tumble drying

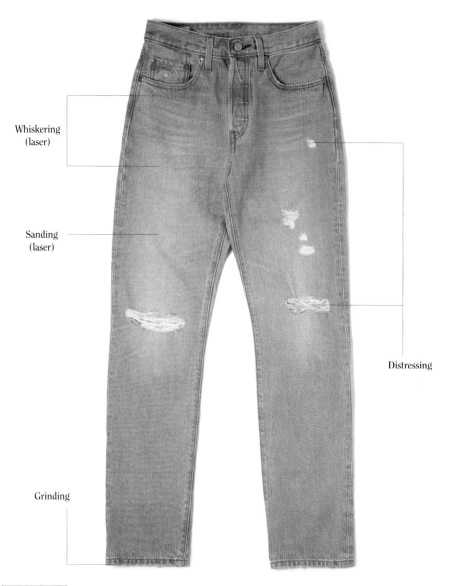

Whiskering
(laser)

Sanding
(laser)

Distressing

Grinding

KEY STEPS

01	02	03	04	05	06	07	08	09
Laser distressing	Desizing	Stone washing	Bleach washing	Neutralizing	Tumble drying	Dry process Grinding, distressing	Rinsing	Tumble drying

KEY STEPS

01	02	03	04	05	06	07
Desizing	Bleach washing	Acid washing	Neutralizing	Rinsing	Tinting	Tumble drying

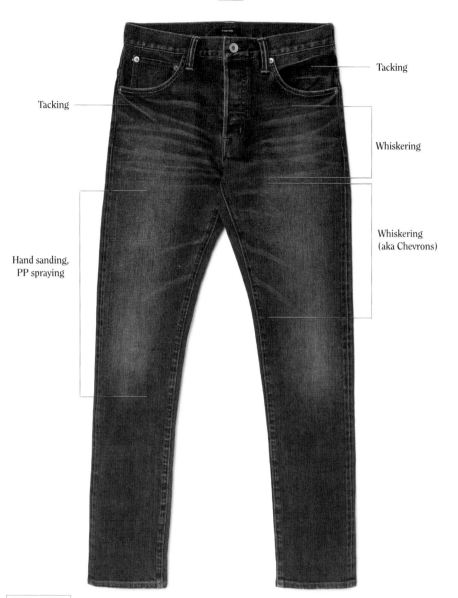

Tacking

Tacking

Whiskering

Whiskering
(aka Chevrons)

Hand sanding,
PP spraying

KEY STEPS

01	02	03	04	05	06	07	08	09
Dry process Hand sanding, whiskering, tacking	**Desizing**	**Enzyme washing**	**Bleach washing** Short cycle	**Tumble drying**	**Dry process** PP spraying	**Neutralizing**	**Rinsing**	**Tumble drying**

Grinding

Whiskering

Ripped and repaired

PP spraying

Grinding

KEY STEPS

01 Dry process Hand sanding, grinding	02 Dipping in resin solution	03 Placing on 3D bendable leg	04 Whiskering Hand scraping	05 Curing in oven	06 Desizing	07 Enzyme washing	08 Bleach washing Short cycle
09 Tumble drying	10 Dry process PP spraying	11 Neutralizing	12 Rinsing	13 Tinting	14 Tumble drying	15 Sewing patches Ripped and repaired areas	

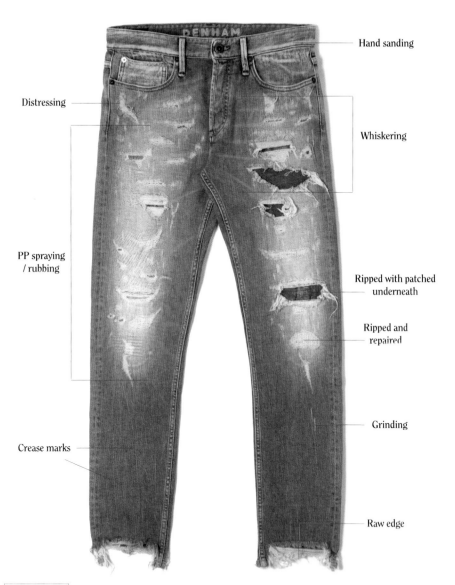

Hand sanding

Distressing

Whiskering

PP spraying / rubbing

Ripped with patched underneath

Ripped and repaired

Grinding

Crease marks

Raw edge

KEY STEPS					
01 **Dry process** Hand sanding, whiskering, adding crease marks, cutting hem	02 **Desizing**	03 **Stone washing**	04 **Bleach washing**	05 **Tumble drying**	06 **Dry process** Grinding, distressing, PP spraying / rubbing
07 **Neutralizing**	08 **Rinsing**	09 **Tumble drying**	10 **Sewing patches** Ripped and repaired areas	11 **Rinsing**	12 **Tumble drying**

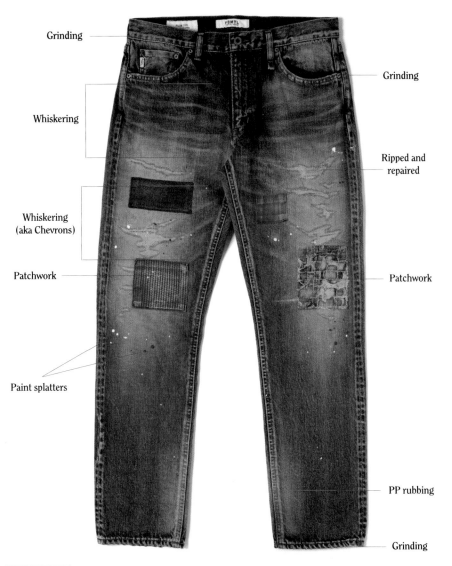

Grinding

Grinding

Whiskering

Ripped and
repaired

Whiskering
(aka Chevrons)

Patchwork

Patchwork

Paint splatters

PP rubbing

Grinding

KEY STEPS						
01 **Dry process** Hand sanding, whiskering, grinding	02 **Desizing**	03 **Enzyme stone washing**	04 **Bleach washing**	05 **Tumble drying**	06 **Dry process** Distressing, adding patchwork, PP spraying/ rubbing	07 **Neutralizing**
08 **Rinsing**	09 **Tinting**	10 **Tumble drying**	11 **Adding patchwork** Ripped and repaired areas	12 **Rinsing**	13 **Tumble drying**	14 **Adding paint splatters**

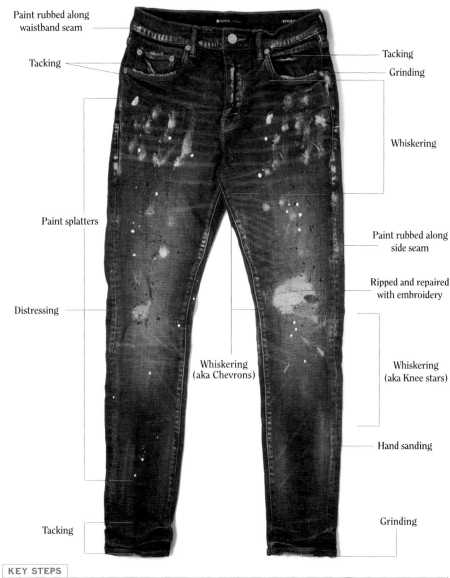

Paint rubbed along waistband seam

Tacking

Tacking

Grinding

Whiskering

Paint splatters

Paint rubbed along side seam

Ripped and repaired with embroidery

Distressing

Whiskering (aka Chevrons)

Whiskering (aka Knee stars)

Hand sanding

Tacking

Grinding

KEY STEPS

01 **Dry process** Hand sanding, whiskering, tacking, grinding	02 **Desizing**	03 **Enzyme washing**	04 **Tumble drying**	05 **Dry process** Distressing, PP spraying and rubbing
06 **Neutralizing**	07 **Rinsing**	08 **Tinting**	09 **Tumble drying**	10 **Adding patches and embroidery** Ripped and repaired areas	11 **Adding pigment splatters and rubbing**

Pigment spray

Grinding

Distressing

Pigment
spraying

PP spraying
/ rubbing

Pigment
splatters

Whiskering
(aka Chevrons)

Resin

KEY STEPS						
01 **Dry process** Hand sanding, whiskering, grinding	02 **Desizing**	03 **Enzyme stone washing**	04 **Bleach washing**	05 **Tumble drying**	06 **Dry process** Grinding, distressing, PP spraying / rubbing	07 **Neutralizing**
08 **Rinsing**	09 **Ozone washing** Bleaching	10 **Pigment spraying**	11 **Rinsing**	12 **Adding pigment splatters**	13 **Spray resin on hem and create creases**	14 **Curing in oven**

Grinding

Tacking

Distressing

Whiskering

Paint splatters

Raw edge

Distressing

KEY STEPS

01 **Dry process** Hand sanding, tacking, whiskering, grinding, cutting hem	02 **Desizing**	03 **Enzyme stone washing**	04 **Bleach washing**	05 **Tumble drying**
06 **Dry process** Distressing, PP spraying	07 **Neutralizing**	08 **Rinsing**	09 **Tinting**	10 **Tumble drying**	11 **Adding pigment splatters**

Grinding

3D whiskers

KEY STEPS

01	02	03	04	05	06	07	08
Dry process Hand sanding	**Dipping in resin solution**	**Placing on 3D bendable leg**	**Whiskering** Hand scraping	**Curing in oven**	**Desizing**	**Bleach washing** Very short cycle	**Tumble drying**

09	10	11	12	13	14	15	16	17
Dry process Grinding, PP spraying	**Neutralizing**	**Rinsing**	**Tumble drying**	**Adding pigment spray**	**Curing in oven**	**Cutting hem**	**Rinsing**	**Tumble drying**

Grinding

Whiskering

Heavily distressed hem

Distressing

Paint splatters

KEY STEPS

01 **Dry process** Hand sanding, whiskering, cutting hem	02 Desizing	03 Enzyme washing	04 Bleach washing	05 Tumble drying
06 **Dry process** Grinding, distressing, PP spraying	07 Neutralizing	08 Rinsing	09 Tinting	10 **Heavily distressing hem** 11 **Adding pigment splatters**

Tacking

Whiskering

Raw edge

PP spraying,
hand sanding

KEY STEPS

01	02	03	04	05	06	07	08	09	10
Dry process Hand sanding, tacking, whiskering, cutting hem	**Desizing**	**Enzyme stone washing** Few stones	**Bleach washing**	**Tumble drying**	**Dry process** PP spraying	**Neutralizing**	**Rinsing**	**Tinting**	**Tumble drying**

DENIM
Garment
DYEING

Garment dyeing – adding or changing the color
of a garment by immersing it in a dye solution
– is performed on a finished item of clothing. In
addition to achieving a wide range of shades, the
method can result in unique patterns. It is best to
use cotton clothing for garment dyeing, as it offers
better absorption.

PAGE — PAGE
166 — 181

GARMENT DYEING, STEP BY STEP

PREADING	>>	FINISHED GARMENT

PREPARATION

FINISHED GARMENT

e.g. desizing, scouring, bleaching (not needed
for Prepared for Dyeing – PFD fabrics)

01 *Optional*
TYING OR FOLDING

02
DYEING / By hand or machine

03
FIXING / Locks in the color

04
RINSING / Removes residual dye

05 *Optional*
SOFTENING / Makes the fabric
smooth and pliable

06
EXTRACTING / Removes water

COMMON DYEING TECHNIQUES

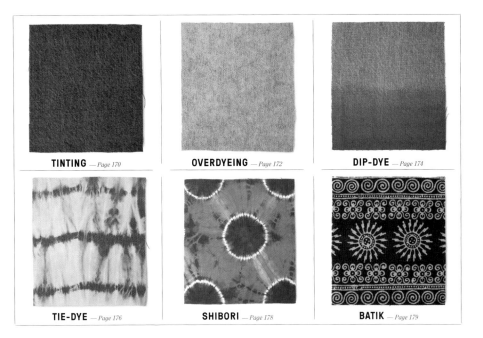

TINTING — *Page 170*

OVERDYEING — *Page 172*

DIP-DYE — *Page 174*

TIE-DYE — *Page 176*

SHIBORI — *Page 178*

BATIK — *Page 179*

COMMON TYPES OF DYE

	LONG-LASTING COLOR **REACTIVE DYE**	FADING COLOR **PIGMENT DYE**	FOR TINTING **DIRECT DYE**
Color	Wide color range. Solid, consistent colors.	Wide color range.	Duller color, especially after washing.
Colorfastness	Good (dye forms strong bond with fiber)	Poor	Poor (color fades and changes easily).
Properties	Water soluble. Comes in powder, liquid or paste form. Application requires less time and lower temperatures.	Not water soluble. Requires pigment dispersion, as well as softener in the last step.	Water soluble. Mostly used for tinting denim clothing. Direct dye has an affinity for fibers and is easily absorbed.
Price	Expensive	Inexpensive	Inexpensive
Common applications	Retains color after many washes. Can be applied to PFD fabrics to produce colored denim.	Used on PFD fabrics for colored denim. Produces an aged and faded look after washing.	Used on indigo denim. Color looks vintage.

TINTING

Tinting is a type of overdyeing that is generally applied to garments, not fabric or yarn. Tinting uses very little dyestuff (around 0.002%), and is usually carried out after the wash processes.

EFFECTS

Alters the hue / cast / tone of indigo and covers it, producing a slight change in appearance as well as a vintage, muddy look.

ORIGINAL
Raw denim

GREEN CAST
Green tint on indigo denim

GRAY CAST
Gray tint on indigo denim

BROWN CAST
Brown tint on indigo denim

RED CAST
Red tint on indigo denim

TIPS

Tinted and sulfur-bottom denim looks identical on the surface. If the back of the denim is colored, the color has been achieved by tinting; if it's white, the denim has a sulfur bottom. That's because tinting is a form of garment dyeing, while sulfur bottom is a type of yarn dyeing.

PROCESS

FULL COVERAGE

STEP 1 Soak the whole garment in a dye bath with weak dye. (By hand or machine)

STEP 2 The garment absorbs the color.

SPOT COVERAGE

STEP 1 Spray the dye on areas of the garment.

STEP 2 The garment is partly colored.

TINTING VS. OVERDYEING

TINTING		OVERDYEING
Weak: around 0.002%	**Strength of dye**	Strong: around 8%
· Slightly colored · Changes the hue / cast / tone of indigo	**Appearance**	· Saturated color · The color almost covers the indigo
Used, vintage, softly colored look	**Effect**	Colored-denim look

OVERDYE

Soaking a garment in a dye bath creates a unique color.
The process uses more dyestuff than tinting does.

OVERDYEING PFD TWILL

EFFECTS
Adds a strong
overtone to the
base color.

ORIGINAL
PFD twill

If pigment dyes are used, the overdyed
color will disappear gradually and the
color of the original fabric will begin to
re-emerge, revealing a unique shade.

OVERDYED
PFD twill overdyed in gray (reactive dyes are used)

PROCESS

STEP 1 Soak the whole
garment in a dye bath
with strong dye. (By
hand or machine)

STEP 2 The garment
absorbs the color.

OVERDYEING INDIGO DENIM

ORIGINAL
Raw denim

COLOR OVERDYE
Acid washing is done before overdyeing;
this is a pink overdye.

BLACK OVERDYE
Indigo denim overdyed black.

WHAT IS PFD FABRIC?
Prepared for dyeing. off-white PFD fabrics are specially treated to
take dyes very well and very evenly.

WHY USE PFD FABRIC INSTEAD OF WHITE DENIM FOR MAKING COLORED DENIM?
White denim contains optical brighteners that, chemically, take up the
same space as dye. This makes it difficult to achieve dark shades, and the
brighteners can dull the color.

DIP-DYE

Dip-dyeing creates a color gradient on a garment.
Part of a garment is dipped into a dye bath or bleach solution. The darkness of the color
depends on the strength of the dye and the immersion time.

DIP-DYEING PFD TWILL

ORIGINAL
PFD twill

> **EFFECTS**
> Two or more
> gradient colors, or
> multiple layers of
> color on a single
> garment.

DARK BLUE DIP-DYE
Half of the PFD garment is dipped in dark blue dye.

PROCESS: ONE COLOR

STEP 1 Hold the garment
over the dye bath and
only submerge the area
to be dyed (or bleached).

STEP 2 The top will not be
affected; the rest will absorb
the dye (or bleach).

DIP-DYEING INDIGO DENIM

ORIGINAL
Raw denim

Bleached

BLEACH DIP
Dip part of the garment in bleach.

Dip-dyed (darker blue)

INDIGO DIP-DYE
Lightly bleach the whole garment, then dip part of it in dark blue dye.

Dip-dyed (green)

Bleached

BLEACH DIP+COLOR DIP-DYE
Bleach part of the garment; then dip most of the bleached part in dye, leaving a small band of the fabric undyed.

PROCESS: GRADIENT COLORS

Dip-dye multiple times for a gradient of 3 or more colors.

STEP 1

Dip Area

STEP 2

Dip Area

Dip Area

STEP 3

Dip Area

Dip Area

TIE-DYE

A type of resist dyeing, tie-dyeing creates patterns by twisting, folding or wrinkling a garment then binding it before dyeing. The tightly bound areas will remain undyed, while the rest of the garment will absorb the dye, leaving distinctive marks and patterns. Shibori is a type of traditional Japanese tie-dye; the process is different from Western-style tie-dye.

TIE-DYEING PFD TWILL

ORIGINAL
PFD twill

TIE-DYED
Dip 2/3 of the PFD twill in pale blue dye. Then, dip half of the pale blue area in darker blue dye. Dip the remaining 1/3 in peach dye.

PROCESS

STEP 1 Fold areas of the garment and bind them tightly with string or rubber bands.

STEP 2 Soak all or part of the garment in a dye/bleach bath.

STEP 3 Remove from dye and take off binding.

TIE-DYEING INDIGO DENIM

ORIGINAL
Raw denim

Bound, unbleached area

Bound, unbleached area

Bound area untouched
by bleach or dye

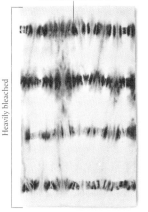

Heavily bleached

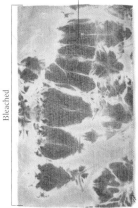

Bleached

Heavily bleached

Dyed (orange) area

BLEACH TIE-DYE
Garment is soaked in a strong
bleach bath.

BLEACH TIE-DYE
Garment is soaked in a low- to medium-
strength bleach bath.

BLEACH + COLOR TIE-DYE
After binding areas of the garment, soak
it in a strong bleach bath. Unbind; bind
different areas, then soak the garment in
a dye bath.

STORY

Tie-dye originated in China and Japan, then
rose to popularity in the United States in the
1920s. It reached its peak in the US with the
hippie movement of the 1960s, becoming
synonymous with counterculture, Woodstock,
the Summer of Love and psychedelia.

SHIBORI

Shibori, from the Japanese verb meaning "to wring, squeeze or press," is a manual resist-dyeing technique using indigo dye. Fabric is folded, pleated, bound or stitched, then submerged in a dye bath. The tightly bound areas remain untouched, while the rest of the fabric absorbs the dye, producing patterns.

ORIGINAL
White cotton muslin

AFTER NE-MAKI

STORY

The oldest shibori pieces found in Japan seem to be Chinese imports. The 17th through 19th centuries (the Edo period in Japan) saw the peak of shibori production. The elite classes were permitted to wear silk, so the lower classes turned to wearing decorative shibori textiles.

PROCESS

STEP 1 Tie, bind or stitch the garment in small areas.

STEP 2 Soak the bound garment in a dye bath.

STEP 3 Dry and unbind the garment.

BATIK

This traditional Indonesian wax-resist dyeing method is usually done by hand, and results in delicate and intricate patterns.
Melted wax is drawn, painted or stamped onto fabric before dyeing. The waxed areas remain untouched, while the rest of the fabric absorbs the dye.

ORIGINAL
Cotton calico

EFFECTS
Intricate hand-drawn or stamped patterns. The artistic possibilities are endless, and batik can be done in a single color or multiple colors.

STORY
The word batik is derived from the Javanese word *ambatik*; *amba* means to write, and *titik* means dot or point.

AFTER

PROCESS

STEP 1 Draw, brush or stamp liquefied wax onto a garment or piece of fabric.

STEP 2 Soak the garment in a dye bath.

STEP 3 Remove the wax with hot water or a solvent.

A COMPARISON OF RESIST-DYEING TECHNIQUES

NE-MAKI

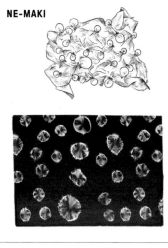

ITAJIME

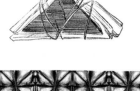
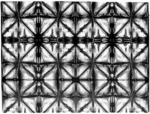

SHIBORI

- One of oldest indigo resist-dyeing techniques in Japan.
- Thread or yarn is used to bind pinched, gathered or folded fabric before dyeing.

- A far more intricate process than tie-dye.
- Produces artistic or uneven patterns.
- Traditionally, indigo dye is used.

ARASHI

ORI-NUI

CRUMPLE

SPIRAL

TIE-DYE

· A popular Western form of resist-dyeing.
· Uses simple materials such as rubber bands or string to bind folded, twisted, or pleated fabric before dyeing.

· Many patterns can be achieved including spirals, bull's-eyes, stripes or squares.
· Technique lends itself to vivid colors and multicolored patterns.

STRIPES

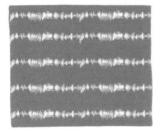

SQUARES

CHAPTER
6

... THE ...

DENIM

Maintenance
GUIDE

Denim clothing has a tendency to fade. Improper
washing methods can cause shrinkage and
unintended severe fading.

Most denim brands provide care labels inside the
clothing for consumers to follow. Some people
prefer to wash denim frequently, while others
never wash it. Follow guidelines for maintaining,
washing and storing denim to give it a long life.

PAGE — PAGE
182 — 193

TO WASH *OR* NOT TO WASH?

Denim jeans are not like regular clothes. Every time denim is washed it loosens or shrinks, and the indigo dye fades a bit. Therefore, how you maintain and wash your denim clothing is important.

MAINTENANCE

Denim lovers prefer not to wash their jeans. This helps preserve the original color, contrast, shape and wear marks. There are ways to maintain a denim garment without actually laundering it, while still preventing odors and bacteria, and removing stains.

WASHING

From a scientific perspective, washing denim more frequently can help prevent bacteria and odors, and keep your skin clean. Many brands include care labels for customers. These methods can minimize unwanted fading and shrinkage.

NO MATTER WHICH CLEANING METHOD YOU USE, REMEMBER:

**DO NOT
TUMBLE DRY**

**DO NOT
USE BLEACH**

**DO NOT PRESS HARD
WHEN IRONING**

HOW TO MAINTAIN DENIM

Most odors are caused by a combination of bacteria, humidity and heat.
The key to keeping denim odor-free without washing is to spot-treat any stains
immediately, and dry it thoroughly.

1. SPOT CLEAN

Gently treat small stains with warm water and a
small amount of denim detergent, rather than
washing the entire pair of jeans.

2. DEODORIZE

Use a deodorizer or antibacterial spray that's
designed specifically for denim. This will hinder
the growth of odor-causing bacteria.

3. KEEP DRY

Keep jeans as dry as possible by using a
dehumidifier or hanging them outdoors.
This will help prevent odors caused by sweat,
dirt and bacteria.

HOW TO WASH DENIM

To prolong the life of denim garments, it is important to follow the manufacturer's care instructions. Doing so will preserve the original indigo dye and help your clothes last longer.

1. WASH INFREQUENTLY

Only wash jeans every 4 to 6 wears, or until they start to smell. Washing them less frequently helps maintain their original color, stretch and fit.

2. WASH SEPARATELY

Wash denim clothing separately from other clothes – especially red and white garments – to prevent their dyes from bleeding and staining.

3. TURN IT INSIDE OUT

Turn your jeans inside out and fasten them before washing to prevent excessive fading. Use a gentle setting to maintain fit and minimize damage to the fabric.

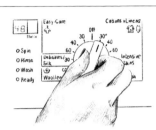

4. WASH IN COLD

Launder denim in cold water. This will help maintain the color, and keep it from fading and shrinking.

> Some people use a hot wash to shrink and fade their denim clothing.

HAND WASH

Soak the denim in a vat or bathtub with a little detergent (ideally denim detergent); agitate the water by hand. Leave the denim to soak for around 30 minutes, then rinse in clean, cold water.

MACHINE WASH

For machine washing, use cold water, a gentle setting, and only a small amount of detergent (ideally denim detergent). Make sure there's no chlorine in the detergent.

5. LINE-DRY

Hang denim, or lay it flat to dry. Avoid direct sunlight to prevent fading.

HOW TO REMOVE STAINS

Treating a stain as soon as it happens can keep it from penetrating the fabric.
Particularly tough stains can be more difficult to remove without fading the denim.

RUST

STEP 1 Lay the jeans flat on a towel.
2 Saturate the stained area with warm white
vinegar and lemon juice.
3 Blot up the excess liquid with a towel.
4 Rinse the jeans with cold water.

RED WINE

STEP 1 Blot up the excess liquid.
2 Place a clean towel under the stain.
3 Cover the stain with salt. Let the salt soak up
the moisture until the fabric is dry.

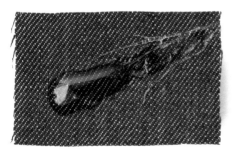

SUPERGLUE

STEP 1 Allow the superglue to dry.
2 Wet a towel with acetone nail-polish remover
and blot the stained area for about a minute.
3 Scrub the stained area with an old toothbrush
until the glue starts to flake off.

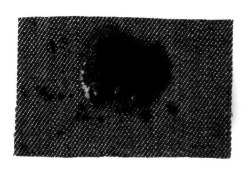

COFFEE

STEP 1 Blot up the excess liquid.
2 Soak the stained area with a mixture of warm water, mild detergent and white vinegar for 15 minutes.
3 Use a sponge and rubbing alcohol to blot up any residue.

INK

STEP 1 Place a clean towel under the stain.
2 Pour 90% rubbing alcohol – or spray hairspray – directly onto the stain.
3 Blot the stain with a clean towel until it disappears.
4 Rinse the jeans in cold water to remove the cleaning substances.

MOTOR OIL

STEP 1 When the jeans are dry, apply a drop of degreaser to a hidden area to test; wait a minute to see if there are any changes.
2 Apply the degreaser directly to the stain and work it in for 3-5 minutes.
3 Using a few drops of detergent, rub the stain for another 5 minutes.
4 Rinse with warm water.

HOW TO REMOVE STAINS

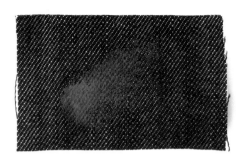

LIPSTICK

STEP 1 Remove the excess lipstick.
2 Brush the stained area with rubbing alcohol
and hot water.
3 Blot dry with a paper towel.
4 Rinse with cool water.

TOMATO SAUCE

STEP 1 Soak the stained area with white vinegar
for 5 minutes.
2 Rinse with cold water.

CHOCOLATE

STEP 1 Gently blot the stained area with a solution
of a mild detergent and water.
2 Blot the stain again with 1/4 cup of white
vinegar (or baking soda) mixed with 3/4 water.
3 Apply the detergent solution once more if the
stain remains visible.
4 Rinse with warm water.

GRASS

STEP 1 Soak the jeans in cold water for 30 minutes.
2 Mix a solution of white vinegar and warm water.
3 Saturate the stained area by dabbing the solution on with a
clean towel and allowing it to sit for 5 minutes.
4 Massage chlorine-free detergent into the stain with a brush
for a few minutes, and allow it to sit for 10-15 minutes.
5 Rinse the jeans with cold water.

PAINT

For acrylic, latex, water-based paints
STEP 1 Scrape off the paint with a knife if it's still fresh.
2 Scrape the stained area with a towel soaked in warm water.
3 Soak the stained area in rubbing alcohol.
4 Using an old toothbrush, scrub off as much
of the paint as you can.

For oil-based paints
STEP 1 Place a clean towel on the stain.
2 Pour paint thinner or turpentine on the back of
the stain to loosen it from the fabric.
3 Rinse with warm water and repeat if there's any residue.

BLOOD

For fresh blood
Soak a clean towel in cold water and wipe the stain
immediately until the fabric is clean.

For dried blood
STEP 1 Scrub the stain in cold water with a few drops of
mild detergent.
2 Mix salt, baking soda or ammonia with water and blot
the stain if there's any residue.

HOW TO STORE DENIM

Storing your denim incorrectly can cause it to fade, crease and lose its shape.
The safe storage methods below are used by many denim brands in their stores,
and can also be used at home.

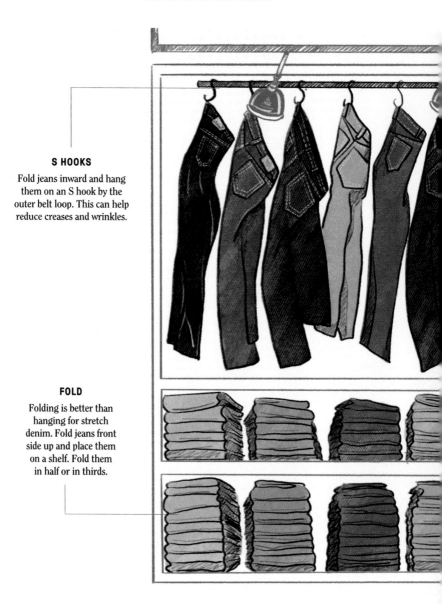

S HOOKS

Fold jeans inward and hang
them on an S hook by the
outer belt loop. This can help
reduce creases and wrinkles.

FOLD

Folding is better than
hanging for stretch
denim. Fold jeans front
side up and place them
on a shelf. Fold them
in half or in thirds.

*IMPORTANT POINTS

Avoid using hanger clips with sharp metal teeth. They can leave lasting marks or even damage fabric.

HANG

Fold the jeans over the bar of a hanger or on a trouser rack. Alternatively, hang denim clothing on hangers using clips.*

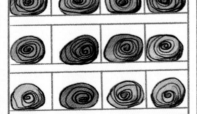

ROLL

Roll the jeans along the seams (from waist to hem). This method keeps denim crease-free.

SHADES OF DENIM

ACKNOWLEDGMENTS

Chairman
PENTER YIP

Editor in Chief
MANGO LEUNG

Editors
MINNIE LAM
SARA CHOW
JANE KWAN

Book Designer
SAUMAN WONG

Illustrator
VIKKI YAU

Photographer
LAMMY CHAN

Copy Editor & Proofreader
LISA BURNETT HILLMAN

Consultants
KEN KO
OSMOND LEE

Contributors
We would like to thank all the contributors who gave us
their professional information and feedback, and helped us
make improvements to this book.

DR. JOSHUA LAW	HERMAN WONG	KIT WONG
RONNIE TUNG	SAMUEL CHOW	FAT TSE
KARMUEL YOUNG	TOMMY LI	RAE LAI
PAUL HO	THOMAS SIT	BOWIE WONG
TOBY NG	RAY CHAN	JACKY WONG

CREDITS

SAMPLES BY

⟨ BASE WEALTH LIMITED ⟩

DENIM FABRIC
EMAIL: **info@basewealth.com.hk**

Base Wealth Limited, established in 1993, manufactures, produces and exports
high-quality denim in the US, the EU, Japan, China and Hong Kong. To cope
with a rapidly changing industry, the company works closely with raw material
suppliers in employing state-of-the-art technology to deliver the best-quality
denim on the market.

⟨ YUEN HING COTTON COMPANY LIMITED ⟩

RECYCLED COTTON/ YARN/ DENIM FABRIC
WEBSITE: **yhccl.com**

Yuen Hing has more than 40 years' experience producing denim, spinning yarn,
and collecting and processing recycled cotton. The company's raw material
supply chain is located in Asia, with headquarters in Hong Kong and factories
in mainland China and Vietnam. Yuen Hing obtained the world's first Global
Recycled Standard (GRS) certification for its recycled cotton fibers and yarns.
The company is committed to using sustainable materials to produce fabrics while
also maintaining quality and stability.

LAI SHUN WASHING AND DYEING COMPANY LIMITED

DENIM WASHING / DYEING
EMAIL: **admin@laishun.com.hk**

Lai Shun, established in 2003, has a wealth of experience in professional denim washing and dyeing techniques, and prioritizes quality and consumer satisfaction. All products are sourced and produced in Hong Kong, and the company's focus is on reaching a global audience and working with world-renowned brands.

JEANOLOGIA

SUSTAINABLE TEXTILE SOLUTIONS
WEBSITE: **jeanologia.com**

Jeanologia, founded in 1994, has become a world leader in sustainable and efficient finishing technologies for textiles; 35% of the jeans in the world are produced with Jeanologia technology, including lasers. Its disruptive technologies help reduce water use, energy consumption, emissions and waste, guaranteeing zero contamination. The company is a shining example of efficiency, ecology and ethics.

NI-MES DENIM FACTORY WORKSHOP

DENIM RENOVATION
INSTAGRAM: **@nimes_deniming**
EMAIL: **jeansworker@gmail.com**

Ni-mes Denim Factory Workshop (Man Fong (Tommy) Li) is a UK-based business that provides professional denim repair, sewing, patching and finishing (washing). The workshop was founded to update and restore old denim, which in turn helps the environment.

TINDY LABELS PRINTING LIMITED

GARMENT ACCESSORIES
EMAIL: **bowie@tindylabels.com**

Tindy, established in 2005, specializes in the design and production of garment labels and accessories. The company has extensive experience in the clothing industry, and has an office in Hong Kong and a factory in mainland China.

REFERENCES

> BOOKS

GLOBAL DENIM
Daniel Miller & Sophie Woodward, Bloomsbury Publishing

DENIM: MANUFACTURE, FINISHING AND APPLICATIONS
Roshan Paul, Woodhead Publishing

JEANS: A CULTURAL HISTORY OF AN AMERICAN ICON
James Sullivan, Gotham

LEVI STRAUSS & CO. (IMAGES OF AMERICA: CALIFORNIA)
Lynn Downey, Arcadia Publishing

DENIM: AN AMERICAN LEGEND
Iain Finlayson, Fireside

**DENIM: FROM COWBOYS TO CATWALKS,
A VISUAL HISTORY OF THE WORLD'S MOST LEGENDARY FABRIC**
Graham Marsh & Paul Trynka, Aurum Press

DENIM: THE FABRIC OF OUR LIVES
Philip Cosker & Zoë Cosker & Hub
Sleaford: Hub, National Centre For Craft And Design

INDIGO: THE COLOR THAT CHANGED THE WORLD
Catherine Legrand, Thames & Husdon

INDIGO
Jenny Balfour-Paul, Archetype Publications

A HANDBOOK OF INDIGO DYEING
Vivien Prideaux, Search Press

DENIM: FASHION'S FRONTIER
Emma McClendon & Fred Dennis, Yale University Press

FASHION FIBERS: DESIGNING FOR SUSTAINABILITY
Annie Gullingsrud, Fairchild Books

THE WORLD TRADE ORGANIZATION AND INTERNATIONAL DENIM TRADING
Yan Li, Y. Shen, L. Yao and E. Newton, Woodhead Publishing

PRINCIPLES OF TEXTILE FINISHING
Asim Kumar Roy Choudhury, Woodhead Publishing

TEXTILE DESIGN: PRINCIPLES, ADVANCES AND APPLICATIONS
A Briggs-Goode, K Townsend, Woodhead Publishing

THE BERG COMPANION TO FASHION
Valerie Steele, Bloomsbury Publishing

STREET STYLE IN AMERICA: AN EXPLORATION
Jennifer Grayer Moore, Greenwood

ENCYCLOPEDIC DICTIONARY OF TEXTILE TERMS: VOLUME 3
Kolanjikombil Matthews, WPI Publishing

THE OLD WEST IN FACT AND FILM: HISTORY VERSUS HOLLYWOOD
Jeremy Agnew, McFarland & Company

デニム・バイブル
田中敦子 訳
株式会社ブルース・インターアクションズ

牛仔褲：叛逆、狂野與性感的自我表述
BLUE JEANS: VOM LEBEN IN STOFFEN UND BILDERN
Anna Schober, 陳素幸 譯
藍鯨出版社

從工作褲到時尚單品：LEVI'S 501XX牛仔褲的誕生
青田充宏, 王美娟 譯
萬里機構

牛仔布和牛仔服裝實用手冊
梅自強
中國紡織出版社

牛仔服裝的設計加工與後整理
香港理工大學紡織及製衣學系, 香港服裝產品開發與行銷研究中心
中國紡織出版社出版社

MAGAZINES

ALL ABOUT VINTAGE DENIM
LIGHTNING MAGAZINE VOL.91, JAPANESE EDITION
エイ出版社

WEBSITES

allure.com

apoormansmillions.com

batikguild.org.uk

bbc.com

biofriendlyplanet.com

byrdie.com

carhartt.com

cleaning.tips.net

cottonmill.com

denim-fever.net

denim.premierevision.com

denimdudes.co

denimhunters.com

denimology.com

denimsandjeans.com

dyeingworld1.blogspot.com

eatsleepdenim.com

edition.cnn.com

esquire.com

fashionista.com

fashionpathfinder.tokyo

fibre2fashion.com

fireflyandfinch.com

flashbak.com

fortune.com

foxnewspoint.com

garmentswashing.blogspot.com

gbmoven.com

gearpatrol.com

gq-magazine.co.uk

grailed.com

heddels.com

historyofjeans.com

ikfoundation.org

insider.com

instyle.com

ispo.com

jeanologia.com

jeansmuseum.org

jmecustomjeans.com

lee.com

levi-strauss-museum.de

levistrauss.com

long-john.nl

luxatic.com

madetoorderjeans.com

marieclaire.com

mercurynews.com

modernfarmer.com

mymodernmet.com

nzfashionmuseum.org.nz

okayama-japan.jp

ordnur.com

oureverydaylife.com

purewow.com

researchgate.net

rockmount.com

sewguide.com

slate.com

smithsonianmag.com

sourcingjournal.com

stylejeanswear.com

sundaypost.com

textileaid.blogspot.com

textileapex.blogspot.com

textilestudycenter.com

textiletoday.com.bd

the-spin-off.com

thedenimeye.com

theguardian.com

thestreet.com

underthemoonlight.ca

usatoday.com

vintagedancer.com

vogue.fr

vox.com

wikihow.com

williamsburggarment.com

ykkfastening.com